REA's *interactive Flashcards*™

ECONOMICS

**Staff of Research and Education Association,
Dr. M. Fogiel, Director**

 Research & Education Association
61 Ethel Road West
Piscataway, New Jersey 08854

REA's INTERACTIVE FLASHCARDS™ ECONOMICS

Printed in the United States of America

Library of Congress Catalog Card Number 98-67209

International Standard Book Number 0-87891-155-3

Research & Education Association, Piscataway, New Jersey 08854

REA's Interactive Flashcards

What they're for

How to use them

They come in a book, not in a box of hundreds of loose cards.

They are most useful as test time approaches to help you check your test readiness.

They are a good tool for self-study and also for group study. They can even be used as a competitive game to see who scores best.

They work with any text.

The interactive feature is a unique learning tool. With it, you can write in your own answer to each question which you can then check against the correct answer provided on the flip side of each card.

You will find that the flashcards in a book have several advantages over flashcards in a box.

You don't have to cope with hundreds of loose cards. Whenever you want to study, you don't have to decide beforehand which cards you are likely to need; you don't have to pull them out of a box (and later return them in their proper place). You can just open the book and get going without ado.

To review material in a specific area such as microeconomics or macroeconomics, refer to the table of contents at the front of the book.

A very detailed index will guide you to whatever topics you want to cover.

A number of blank card pages is included, in case you want to construct some of your own Q's and A's.

You can take along REA's Flashcard book anywhere, ready for use when you are. You don't need to tote along the box or a bunch of loose cards.

REA's Flashcard books have been carefully put together with REA's customary concern for quality. We believe you will find them an excellent review and study tool.

Dr. M. Fogiel
Program Director

P.S. As you could tell, you could see all the flashcards in the book while you were in the store; they aren't sealed in shrink-wrap.

CONTENTS

Note: *Numbers in the Table of Contents refer to question numbers.*

MICROECONOMICS

FUNDAMENTALS OF SUPPLY AND DEMAND

CONSUMER THEORY

PRODUCTION—REVENUE AND COST

PERFECT COMPETITION

MONOPOLISTIC COMPETITION AND OLIGOPOLIES

MACROECONOMICS

INTRODUCTION TO ECONOMICS

THE ECONOMIC PROBLEM

DEMAND AND SUPPLY

ECONOMIC SYSTEMS

THE PRIVATE SECTOR OF THE AMERICAN ECONOMY

THE PUBLIC SECTOR OF THE AMERICAN ECONOMY

GROSS NATIONAL PRODUCT

MACROECONOMIC MODELS

THE INCOME-EXPENDITURE MODEL

FISCAL POLICY ISSUES

MONEY AND BANKING

MONETARY POLICY

INFLATION

ECONOMIC GROWTH

INTERNATIONAL ECONOMICS

GENERAL REVIEW QUESTIONS

HOW TO USE THE FLASHCARDS IN THIS BOOK

There are several types of questions that you will encounter in this book. They include true-or-false questions, fill-in-the-blank questions, and short answer questions.

The topics and questions were selected to correspond to levels of difficulty, ranging from the simple and basic to the more advanced.

To review material for a specific topic, refer to the table of contents at the front of the book.

A very detailed index at the end of the book will guide you to whatever topic you want to cover.

The flashcards at the end of the book deal with more advanced topics.

Questions

Q1

What kind of science is economics?

*Your Own Answer*_____

_____

Q2

True or False: Microeconomics focuses on problems of a national or worldwide scale, rather than on problems specific to a household, firm, or industry.

*Your Own Answer*_____

_____

Q3

Which have positive prices: free goods or economic goods?

*Your Own Answer*_____

_____

Correct Answers

A1

Social Science

A2

False. Microeconomics is specific, and macroeconomics is national and worldwide.

A3

Economic goods

Questions

Q4

What are the four factors of production?

*Your Own Answer*_____

_____

Q5

True or False: Money is considered to be an economic resource.

*Your Own Answer*_____

_____

Q6

_____are considered capital goods rather than consumer goods.

*Your Own Answer*_____

_____

Correct Answers

A4

Land, labor, capital, and management (sometimes called entrepreneurial talent)

A5

False. Economists do not consider money as an economic resource.

A6

Examples are: sugar, shirts, engines, microcomputers (engine)

Questions

Q7

What is a capital intensive good?

*Your Own Answer*_____

_____

Q8

What are causes of growth of production?

*Your Own Answer*_____

_____

Q9

True or False: In order to get equal extra amounts of one good, you must give up an ever-increasing amount of another good.

*Your Own Answer*_____

_____

Correct Answers

A7

A good that uses more capital than labor to produce it

A8

Improvement in technology, increase in resource supply, and education

A9

True. Increasing relative costs.

Questions

Q10

True or False: If the input of some resource is increased while others are held constant, output will increase, but at a decreasing rate.

Your Own Answer_____

_____

Q11

If an increase in inputs leads to a less than proportionate increase in outputs, this is known as _____.

Your Own Answer_____

_____

Q12

If an increase in inputs leads to a proportionate increase in outputs, this is known as _____.

Your Own Answer_____

_____

Correct Answers

A10

True. Diminishing returns.

A11

diminishing returns to scale

A12

constant returns to scale

Questions

Q13

When the increase in output is more than proportionate to the increase in input, this is known as _____ .

*Your Own Answer*_____

_____

Q14

True or False: A market is the interaction between potential buyers and sellers of goods and services, where money is usually used as the medium of exchange.

*Your Own Answer*_____

_____

Q15

The quantity of a good that consumers are willing and able to purchase at a certain price is known as the _____ .

*Your Own Answer*_____

_____

Correct Answers

A13

economy of scale

A14

True. Most products are bought or sold for money.

A15

demand

Questions

Q16

True or False: Desire to buy is the same as demand.

*Your Own Answer*_____

_____

Q17

How the quantity demanded of a good changes as the price of that good changes, holding everything else constant, is known as _____ .

*Your Own Answer*_____

_____

Q18

True or False: A normal good describes the following: as the price of a good increases, the quantity demanded of that good falls.

*Your Own Answer*_____

_____

Correct Answers

A16

False. The ability to buy is the same as demand.

A17

demand curve

A18

True

Questions

Q19

True or False: In economics, only price would cause a change in demand.

*Your Own Answer*_____

Q20

True or False: Everything else being equal, an increase in a person's income would cause an increase in quantity demanded.

*Your Own Answer*_____

Q21

True or False: Everything else being equal, an increase in population would cause an increase in quantity demanded.

*Your Own Answer*_____

Correct Answers

A19

False. Other factors, such as consumer income, could cause a change in demand.

A20

True. Increased income usually increases a person's demand for goods.

A21

True. More people, more goods demanded and produced.

Questions

Q22

True or False: Everything else being equal, a shift in consumer tastes in favor of a particular good will cause a decrease in the demand for that good.

*Your Own Answer*_____

Q23

True or False: A decrease in the price of tennis balls causes an increase in the demand for tennis racquets.

*Your Own Answer*_____

Q24

True or False: A decrease in the price of margarine causes an increase in the demand for butter.

*Your Own Answer*_____

Correct Answers

A22

False. More popular, more demand.

A23

True. More of each—increased demand, complementary goods.

A24

False. Substitution effect.

Questions

Q25

True or False: Usually, as the price of a good rises, the quantity supplied rises.

*Your Own Answer*_____

Q26

True or False: If an industry producing the good increases in size, the supply of the good will increase in size.

*Your Own Answer*_____

Q27

True or False: Any technological progress in the production of a good will decrease the supply of that good.

*Your Own Answer*_____

Correct Answers

A25

True

A26

True. Size of industry influences quantity supplied.

A27

False. Technology increases supply.

Questions

Q28

True or False: If the prices of inputs used in the production of goods decrease, the supply of the goods will increase.

*Your Own Answer*_____

Q29

True or False: If the prices of inputs used in the production of goods increase, the supply of the goods will increase.

*Your Own Answer*_____

Q30

If everything else is equal but price drops, _____.

*Your Own Answer*_____

Correct Answers

A28

True. Low price increases quantity.

A29

False. Higher prices usually decrease quantity of goods.

A30

quantity supplied decreases

Questions

Q31

When quantity demanded exceeds quantity supplied, the result is a _____.

*Your Own Answer*_____

_____

Q32

When producers are willing to supply more than consumers are willing to buy, there is a _____.

*Your Own Answer*_____

_____

Q33

If price is the adjusting mechanism to get back to equilibrium, this is known as _____.

*Your Own Answer*_____

_____

Correct Answers

A31

shortage

A32

surplus

A33

Walrasian equilibrium

Questions

Q34

If quantity is the adjusting mechanism to get back to equilibrium, this is known as _____.

*Your Own Answer*_____

Q35

True or False: When market forces are permitted to interact freely, quantity demanded will be higher than quantity supplied and/or quantity demanded will be lower than quantity supplied.

*Your Own Answer*_____

Q36

If demand for a product does not change, no matter what the price, this is known as _____.

*Your Own Answer*_____

Correct Answers

A34

Marshallian equilibrium

A35

False

A36

inelastic demand

Questions

Q37

If demand for a product changes along with changes in price, this is known as _____ .

*Your Own Answer*_____

Q38

True or False: Salt is an example of a product that would probably have an inelastic demand.

*Your Own Answer*_____

Q39

True or False: Along a straight line demand curve, slope is constant, but elasticity changes because slope is an absolute measure and elasticity is a relative measure.

*Your Own Answer*_____

Correct Answers

A37

elastic demand

A38

True

A39

True. Luxuries vs. necessities.

Questions

Q40

True or False: Luxuries would have an inelastic demand while necessities would have an elastic demand.

*Your Own Answer*_____

_____

Q41

True or False: A product with many substitutes would have a more elastic demand than would a product with few substitutes.

*Your Own Answer*_____

_____

Q42

True or False: Consumption is the sole purpose of production.

*Your Own Answer*_____

_____

Correct Answers

A40

False. Vice versa.

A41

True. Elasticity due to substitutes that work as well.

A42

True

Questions

Q43

True or False: In economics it is assumed that the economy's resources are limited and that people's wants are unlimited.

*Your Own Answer*_____

Q44

The Classical Approach to Consumer Demand Theory is _____.

*Your Own Answer*_____

Q45

True or False: Utility is a subjective notion.

*Your Own Answer*_____

Correct Answers

A43

True

A44

cardinal—that is measurement in absolute terms

A45

True

Questions

Q46

True or False: The Marginal Utility Theory assumes that utility is numerically measurable.

*Your Own Answer*_____

_____

Q47

True or False: The rate of change in total utility is called marginal utility.

*Your Own Answer*_____

_____

Q48

True or False: The Law of Diminishing Marginal Utility is that marginal utility decreases as a consumer acquires more units of a certain good.

*Your Own Answer*_____

_____

Correct Answers

A46

True. You need numbers to uphold this theory.

A47

True

A48

True

Questions

Q49

Increased consumption of a good results in _____ adjusted total utility.

*Your Own Answer*_____

_____

Q50

Increased consumption of a good results in a _____ rate of a marginal utility.

*Your Own Answer*_____

_____

Q51

Increased consumption of a good results in _____ marginal utility.

*Your Own Answer*_____

_____

Correct Answers

A49

greater

A50

slower

A51

less

Questions

Q52

True or False: A progressive income tax hits the rich harder than the poor.

*Your Own Answer*_____

Q53

Negatively sloped indifference curves are _____.

*Your Own Answer*_____

Q54

True or False: An example of a complement would be a right sneaker and left sneaker.

*Your Own Answer*_____

Correct Answers

A52

True

A53

downward and to the right

A54

True

Questions

Q55

True or False: An example of a substitute would be butter and margarine.

*Your Own Answer*_____

Q56

If utility (usefulness) is to be kept constant, the less units of A you have, the more units of B must be given in exchange before you will be willing to give up one unit of A. This is known as _____.

*Your Own Answer*_____

Q57

True or False: The marginal utility of a scarcer good is greater relative to the marginal utility of a more abundant good.

*Your Own Answer*_____

Correct Answers

A55

True

A56

The Law of Substitution

A57

True. The last scarce good has more relative value than has the last abundant good.

Questions

Q58

True or False: The saturation point is most relevant when the goods are free of cost.

*Your Own Answer*_____

_____

Q59

True or False: In economics it is assumed that individuals are rational.

*Your Own Answer*_____

_____

Q60

True or False: As the average person becomes wealthier, he or she would probably consume fewer hamburgers.

*Your Own Answer*_____

_____

Correct Answers

A58

True. Free goods aren't desired after awhile.

A59

True. Economics stresses "the rational man."

A60

True

Questions

Q61

True or False: As the price of the good declines, the quantity demanded of that good increases. This is for both normal and inferior goods.

*Your Own Answer*_____

Q62

True or False: The Law of Diminishing Marginal Utility is that the earlier units of the same goods you purchase are of more value than are the final units.

*Your Own Answer*_____

Q63

A process through which resources and/or other products are transformed into different products is called _____.

*Your Own Answer*_____

Correct Answers

A61

True

A62

True

A63

production

Questions

Q64

True or False: The maximum output from given inputs with a given level of technology is called production possibility.

*Your Own Answer*_____

Q65

The least cost production is known as _____.

*Your Own Answer*_____

Q66

True or False: Economic efficiency is closely tied to technical efficiency.

*Your Own Answer*_____

Correct Answers

A64

True

A65

economic efficiency

A66

True

Questions

Q67

True or False: Efficient production assumes that whatever knowledge does exist is being used.

Your Own Answer_____

Q68

True or False: Productivity is the amount of output that is produced by one unit of input.

Your Own Answer_____

Q69

Productivity is measured by units of _____ per unit of _____ .

Your Own Answer_____

Correct Answers

A67

True

A68

True

A69

output; input

Questions

Q70

True or False: In determining productivity, labor is considered part of input.

*Your Own Answer*_____

_____

Q71

Cases in which the percentage increase in output is greater than the percentage increase in input used to produce that output would be known as _____.

*Your Own Answer*_____

_____

Q72

Putting in a less productive input for a more productive input would be known as _____.

*Your Own Answer*_____

_____

Correct Answers

A70

True. Labor and capital are parts of input.

A71

economies of scale

A72

factor substitution

Questions

Q73

Which of the four major factors of production is considered to be the single most important input in the United States?

*Your Own Answer*_____

_____

Q74

A task is broken into specialized tasks, allowing each worker to become more skilled in a particular job. This is known as _____.

*Your Own Answer*_____

_____

Q75

As more workers are hired, more capital is added, but capital per worker remains constant. This is known as _____.

*Your Own Answer*_____

_____

Correct Answers

A73

Labor

A74

division of labor

A75

capital widening

Questions

Q76

Each worker is given more capital input in order to raise productivity—that is, capital per worker increases. This is referred to as _____.

*Your Own Answer*_____

Q77

True or False: The marginal product is the change in output for a unit change of the input.

*Your Own Answer*_____

Q78

True or False: Holding fixed inputs constant and just increasing the one variable input beyond a certain point will result in an increasing marginal product.

*Your Own Answer*_____

Correct Answers

A76

capital deepening

A77

True

A78

False. It will result in decreasing marginal product.

Questions

Q79

The maximum receipts obtainable by selling a given quantity of output per unit of time is known as _____.

*Your Own Answer*_____

Q80

If one divides total revenue by quantity produced, he or she gets _____.

*Your Own Answer*_____

Q81

The change in total revenue caused by one unit change in output sold is called _____.

*Your Own Answer*_____

Correct Answers

A79

total revenue

A80

average revenue

A81

marginal revenue

Questions

Q82

A change in total revenue that results from a one-unit change in some variable input with other inputs held constant is known as _____.

*Your Own Answer*_____

Q83

The value of the alternative that is being given up in order to obtain some specific item is called _____.

*Your Own Answer*_____

Q84

True or False: Economic cost is the same as opportunity cost.

*Your Own Answer*_____

Correct Answers

A82

marginal revenue product

A83

economic cost

A84

True

Questions

Q85

Monetary payments going out of the firm are referred to as _____ .

*Your Own Answer*_____

Q86

Costs associated with the usage of the resources that the firm owns, also called non-expenditures, are referred to as _____ .

*Your Own Answer*_____

Q87

Decrease in the value of a capital good due to wear or obsolescence is called _____ .

*Your Own Answer*_____

Correct Answers

A85

explicit cost

A86

implicit cost

A87

depreciation

Questions

Q88

_____ is an attempt to combine the allocative efficiency of the market with state control of aggregate investment.

_Your Own Answer_____

Q89

Private cost plus any other extraneous cost accrued by members of society, which are infringed on by some trading parties—such as pollution, are referred to as _____.

_Your Own Answer_____

Q90

True or False: A time period not long enough to change all inputs such as plant size, but long enough to change some inputs such as labor, is called short run.

_Your Own Answer_____

Correct Answers

A88

Market socialism

A89

social cost

A90

True

Questions

Q91

True or False: In the long run, all inputs are variable.

Your Own Answer

Q92

True or False: Fixed costs do not vary with the rate of output.

Your Own Answer

Q93

True or False: Fixed costs occur even when output is zero.

Your Own Answer

Correct Answers

A91

True

A92

True

A93

True. Fixed costs such as rent and depreciation continue when output is zero.

Questions

Q94

True or False: Wages are an example of a variable cost.

*Your Own Answer*_____

_____

Q95

True or False: The change in the total cost due to a one-unit change in the rate of output is called marginal cost.

*Your Own Answer*_____

_____

Q96

Is there a law of diminishing marginal productivity or increasing marginal productivity?

*Your Own Answer*_____

_____

Correct Answers

A94

True

A95

True

A96

Diminishing Marginal Productivity

Questions

Q97

True or False: In the long run, all inputs are fixed.

*Your Own Answer*_____

Q98

True or False: In the long run, all inputs are variable.

*Your Own Answer*_____

Q99

True or False: In the short run, some inputs are fixed.

*Your Own Answer*_____

Correct Answers

A97

False. In the long run, all inputs are variable.

A98

True. Most things vary in the long run.

A99

True. Some of these are depreciation and rent.

Questions

Q100

True or False: Plant size is a fixed input in the short run and a variable input in the long run.

Your Own Answer

Q101

Is economics "what businessmen do" or "what economists do"?

Your Own Answer

Q102

Is the study of the economy as a whole considered to be either macroeconomics or microeconomics?

Your Own Answer

Correct Answers

A100

True. Although the building has a limited capacity in the short run, additions can be made to it in the long run.

A101

What economists do

A102

Macroeconomics

Questions

Q103

Is the study of households, business firms, and government agencies considered to be either micro-economics or macroeconomics?

Your Own Answer _____

_____

Q104

Is a set of statements about the cause and effect relationships in the economy a model or a theory?

Your Own Answer _____

_____

Q105

Is an abstract replica of reality considered a theory or a model?

Your Own Answer _____

_____

Correct Answers

A103

Microeconomics

A104

Theory

A105

Model

Questions

Q106

True or False: Models come in verbal, graphical, or mathematical form.

*Your Own Answer*_____

Q107

True or False: Increases in the rate of growth of the money supply will lead to higher inflation.

*Your Own Answer*_____

Q108

True or False: Good empirical analysis does not usually require mastery of sophisticated statistical and mathematical tools.

*Your Own Answer*_____

Correct Answers

A106

True. There are many ways economists can show their ideas.

A107

True. Increased supply makes it worth less.

A108

False. We must have good tools.

Questions

Q109

Do many economists view positive economics as subjective or objective?

Your Own Answer

Q110

Is the analysis of "what should be" considered normative economics or positive economics?

Your Own Answer

Q111

Do economists view normative economics as subjective or objective?

Your Own Answer

Correct Answers

A109

Objective

A110

Normative economics

A111

Subjective

Questions

Q112

True or False: Human needs for goods and services exceed the ability of the economy to satisfy those wants and needs.

*Your Own Answer*_____

Q113

True or False: Individuals never have enough money to buy all they want.

*Your Own Answer*_____

Q114

True or False: Government has enough money to fund all worthwhile projects.

*Your Own Answer*_____

Correct Answers

A112

True. People always want more than they have.

A113

True. Human wants and needs exceed their available income.

A114

False. Citizens always want more from their government.

Questions

Q115

Businesses must make choices, taking some opportunities while foregoing others. Is this idea marginal analysis or opportunity cost?

*Your Own Answer*_____

Q116

True or False: Marginal analysis means that economists assume that people make choices by weighing the costs and benefits of particular actions.

*Your Own Answer*_____

Q117

True or False: Services are tangible items, as are food, cars, and clothing.

*Your Own Answer*_____

Correct Answers

A115

Opportunity cost

A116

True. This is done by consumer choice based on prices.

A117

False. Services are intangible like insurance.

Questions

Q118

Are factories, machinery, and tools considered by economists to be entrepreneurship or capital?

Your Own Answer_____

Q119

Is the ability to detect new business opportunities and bring them to fruition considered to be capital or entrepreneurship?

Your Own Answer_____

Q120

True or False: Human wants and needs are virtually limitless.

Your Own Answer_____

Correct Answers

A118

Capital

A119

Entrepreneurship

A120

True. People always want more than they have.

Questions

Q121

True or False: Resources are plentiful relative to human needs and desires.

*Your Own Answer*_____

Q122

True or False: The typical family in the U.S. is comfortable.

*Your Own Answer*_____

Q123

True or False: The United States is the richest nation in the world.

*Your Own Answer*_____

Correct Answers

A121

False. There are not enough resources to supply wants.

A122

False. The median family income shows that the typical U.S. family does not live comfortably.

A123

True

Questions

Q124

True or False: Under a contributory standard, people making larger contributions receive correspondingly larger shares of goods and services.

*Your Own Answer*_____

Q125

True or False: Under a needs standard, goods and services go to families needing them the most, regardless of contribution.

*Your Own Answer*_____

Q126

True or False: In the production possibilities curve, it is assumed that all resources are used in their most productive manner.

*Your Own Answer*_____

Correct Answers

A124

True

A125

True

A126

True

Questions

Q127

True or False: Economic growth will end the problem of scarcity.

*Your Own Answer*_____

Q128

True or False: People will be able to buy more if the product becomes more expensive.

*Your Own Answer*_____

Q129

True or False: In the supply table, there is generally a positive relationship between price and quantity of supplies, reflecting higher costs associated with greater production.

*Your Own Answer*_____

Correct Answers

A127

False. People will always want more than they have.

A128

False. If prices rise, people buy less.

A129

True. It often costs more per unit to increase supplies.

Questions

Q130

True or False: The word "equilibrium" means the same as "stable".

*Your Own Answer*_____

_____

Q131

Which is probably the good that consumers would want to buy more of if their income rose—hamburger or filet mignon?

*Your Own Answer*_____

_____

Q132

Are bread and butter complements or substitutes?

*Your Own Answer*_____

_____

Correct Answers

A130

True

A131

Filet mignon

A132

Complements

Questions

Q133

True or False: A government mandated level above which a price cannot go is called a price floor.

*Your Own Answer*_____

Q134

Everything else being equal, as technology advances, does the equilibrium price of the products rise or fall?

*Your Own Answer*_____

Q135

If a huge drought is experienced throughout the country, will this cause the price of wheat to rise or fall?

*Your Own Answer*_____

Correct Answers

A133

False. It is called a price ceiling.

A134

Fall

A135

Short supply will cause it to rise.

Questions

Q136

If direct taxes on a product increase, will this cause the equilibrium price of the product to rise or fall?

*Your Own Answer*_____

Q137

Are government mandated rent controls in cities examples of price ceilings or price floors?

*Your Own Answer*_____

Q138

Does a price ceiling cause an artificial surplus or artificial shortage?

*Your Own Answer*_____

Correct Answers

A136

Rise

A137

Price ceilings

A138

Artificial shortage

Questions

Q139

Is the minimum wage law an example of an artificial ceiling or an artificial floor?

*Your Own Answer*_____

Q140

Does a minimum wage law create increased employment or does it cause unemployment?

*Your Own Answer*_____

Q141

True or False: All real-world economies are mixed economies.

*Your Own Answer*_____

Correct Answers

A139

Artificial floor

A140

It causes unemployment.

A141

True. Even China has some private industry along with government industry.

Questions

Q142

True or False: The key characteristic of a capitalistic economy is that productive resources are owned by private individuals.

*Your Own Answer*_____

_____

Q143

True or False: The key characteristic of a socialist economy is that productive resources are owned by private individuals.

*Your Own Answer*_____

_____

Q144

True or False: Economists believe that if certain conditions are met, a market economy is easily capable of achieving the major economic goals.

*Your Own Answer*_____

_____

Correct Answers

A142

True

A143

False. Productive resources in a socialist economy are owned by government.

A144

True. Most people hold that a market economy will help people the most.

Questions

Q145

True or False: A change in taste occurred from men's felt hats to baseball caps, and producers responded to society's desires not out of a sense of public spiritedness, but out of self-interest.

*Your Own Answer*_____

_____

Q146

True or False: In a command economy, business must cater to the whims of consumer tastes or else they will go out of business.

*Your Own Answer*_____

_____

Q147

True or False: In a market economy, the constant struggle for profits will stimulate firms to cut costs.

*Your Own Answer*_____

_____

Correct Answers

A145

True. Higher profits come by providing the public with goods they want.

A146

False. This is an attribute of capitalism.

A147

True. This is part of competition.

Questions

Q148

True or False: In a market economy, technical efficiency of business results from attention to self-interest, not public interest.

*Your Own Answer*_____

Q149

True or False: In a market economy, competition between firms forces them to cater to consumer demands and keep production costs down as far as possible.

*Your Own Answer*_____

Q150

True or False: In a command economy, competition between firms for the consumer's dollar will force a constant search for better products.

*Your Own Answer*_____

Correct Answers

A148

True. Self-interest will profit from satisfying the public.

A149

True. This increases profits.

A150

False. There is little competition in a command economy.

Questions

Q151

True or False: In a market economy, technological change leads to decay and lack of growth of the business.

*Your Own Answer*_____

_____

Q152

True or False: Winners in the market economy are not necessarily the most virtuous of people; they just sell a better product.

*Your Own Answer*_____

_____

Q153

True or False: Those consumers with the most income exert the greatest influence on the pattern of production in a market economy.

*Your Own Answer*_____

_____

Correct Answers

A151

False. Technological change leads to increased profits and growth.

A152

True. People will generally buy better products.

A153

True. People spending more influence production.

Questions

Q154

True or False: In a market economy, high prices indicate that goods and services are in demand.

*Your Own Answer*_____

Q155

True or False: In a market economy, low prices indicate that goods are in demand.

*Your Own Answer*_____

Q156

True or False: In a market economy, low prices indicate plentiful resources.

*Your Own Answer*_____

Correct Answers

A154

True. This is representative of the Law of Supply and Demand.

A155

False. Hard-to-sell goods have lower prices.

A156

True. Great supply of a good tends to lower its price.

Questions

Q157

True or False: Since command economies downplay the role of prices, they have a much easier time achieving allocational and technical efficiency.

Your Own Answer

Q158

True or False: Adam Smith, the founder of modern economics, believed in the command system of economy.

Your Own Answer

Q159

True or False: Adam Smith believed that self-interest was a dominant force in a market economy, yet this self-interest was consistent with the public interest.

Your Own Answer

Correct Answers

A157

False. They have black markets and trouble.

A158

False. He believed in free enterprise.

A159

True

Questions

Q160

True or False: Profits are earned by keeping costs up.

*Your Own Answer*_____

Q161

True or False: Monopolistic businesses increase output and lower prices.

*Your Own Answer*_____

Q162

Is a proprietorship a business form owned by one person or by two persons?

*Your Own Answer*_____

Correct Answers

A160

False. Profits are earned by keeping costs down.

A161

False. Monopolies tend to decrease output and raise prices.

A162

One person

Questions

Q163

Do proprietorship businesses have limited liability or unlimited liability?

Your Own Answer

Q164

True or False: Unlimited liability means that the full debt of a firm becomes the personal responsibility of the proprietor.

Your Own Answer

Q165

True or False: Unlimited life means that the proprietorship business dies when the owner dies.

Your Own Answer

Correct Answers

A163

Unlimited liability

A164

True

A165

False. Unlimited life means that the business lives an indefinite amount of time.

Questions

Q166

True or False: Partnerships have unlimited liability.

*Your Own Answer*_____

Q167

True or False: If your partners leave the country, you may have to cover all of their business debts.

*Your Own Answer*_____

Q168

True or False: Decision-making becomes progressively easier as the number of partners increases.

*Your Own Answer*_____

Correct Answers

A166

True. This is one of the disadvantages of a partnership.

A167

True. A partner's unlimited liability makes you responsible for their debts.

A168

False. It becomes progressively harder for so many partners to agree.

Questions

Q169

True or False: A partnership dies when any of the partners die.

*Your Own Answer*_____

Q170

True or False: Partnerships are harder to start than corporations.

*Your Own Answer*_____

Q171

True or False: Partnerships and corporations need charters.

*Your Own Answer*_____

Correct Answers

A169

True. This is one of the rules of partnership.

A170

False. One of the advantages of partnerships is that they are easy to start.

A171

False. Corporations need charters, but not partnerships.

Questions

Q172

True or False: Corporations raise their initial capital by selling shares of stock.

*Your Own Answer*_____

Q173

Are the stockholders or the bondholders the owners of the corporation?

*Your Own Answer*_____

Q174

True or False: There is virtually no limit to the amount of capital a corporation can raise.

*Your Own Answer*_____

Correct Answers

A172

True. This is the way most corporations start.

A173

Stockholders

A174

True. Corporations are the largest businesses and raise huge amounts of money through the sale of stocks and bonds.

Questions

Q175

True or False: Stockholders have unlimited liability.

*Your Own Answer*_____

_____

Q176

True or False: Corporations can continue even if their initial owners die.

*Your Own Answer*_____

_____

Q177

True or False: Corporations are subject to double taxation.

*Your Own Answer*_____

_____

Correct Answers

A175

False. Stockholders are liable for corporate debts only to the extent of their stock investment.

A176

True. Corporations have unlimited life.

A177

True. The corporations themselves pay income tax, and their dividends are taxable income to stockholders.

Questions

Q178

Is a business firm that competes in two or more unrelated industries called a monopoly or a conglomerate?

*Your Own Answer*_____

_____

Q179

True or False: A group of firms that produce the same product is called an industry.

*Your Own Answer*_____

_____

Q180

True or False: A series of laws that attempts to promote greater competition in the private business sector is called a conglomerate.

*Your Own Answer*_____

_____

Correct Answers

A178

Conglomerate

A179

True. An example is the steel industry.

A180

False. It is called antitrust.

Questions

Q181

Is anything of value that you own called wealth or income?

*Your Own Answer*_____

Q182

True or False: Stock variable is an economic variable that can only be meaningfully measured at a particular point of time.

*Your Own Answer*_____

Q183

What is the difference between an individual's wealth and his debts called?

*Your Own Answer*_____

Correct Answers

A181

Wealth. It provides the owner with goods, services, or money.

A182

True. Stock variable is wealth measured at a particular point in time.

A183

Net worth

Questions

Q184

True or False: Economists consider net worth as one of the stock variables.

*Your Own Answer*_____

_____

Q185

Are goods, services, or money that wealth provides considered to be net worth or income?

*Your Own Answer*_____

_____

Q186

Is income measured at a point in time or over a period of time?

*Your Own Answer*_____

_____

Correct Answers

A184

True. It is wealth at a particular point in time.

A185

Income. Examples are dividends and interest.

A186

Over a period of time, such as a year

Questions

Q187

True or False: An economic variable whose value can only be meaningfully measured over a period of time is known as a flow variable.

*Your Own Answer*_____

Q188

True or False: Income is distributed fairly evenly among households in the United States.

*Your Own Answer*_____

Q189

True or False: The median family income is the average family income.

*Your Own Answer*_____

Correct Answers

A187

True

A188

False. Many people are rich, many more are poor, some are in between.

A189

False. The average is the same as the mean, or the arithmetic average. The median income is the one right in the middle. Half the families make more and half make less.

Questions

Q190

True or False: Wealth as measured by net worth is distributed unequally in the United States.

*Your Own Answer*_____

_____

Q191

In economics, does the public sector refer to large business or to the government?

*Your Own Answer*_____

_____

Q192

True or False: Money-in-kind items given by the government to individuals or businesses, for which the government receives no equivalent good or service in return are called transfer payments.

*Your Own Answer*_____

_____

Correct Answers

A190

True. Some families own hardly anything after all their bills are paid. Others are extremely wealthy.

A191

The government

A192

True. Examples would be: social security payments, welfare payments, unemployment compensation.

Questions

Q193

Is the marginal tax rate the same as the average tax rate?

*Your Own Answer*_____

Q194

True or False: A progressive tax system is one where everyone pays the same tax rate.

*Your Own Answer*_____

Q195

Is a tax system where persons with higher incomes pay a lower average tax rate called regressive or proportional?

*Your Own Answer*_____

Correct Answers

A193

No. The marginal tax rate is the proportion of each additional dollar paid in taxes, while the average tax rate is the proportion of income paid in taxes.

A194

False. A progressive tax system is one where taxpayers with higher incomes pay higher average tax rates.

A195

Regressive

Questions

Q196

True or False: In a regressive tax system, the marginal tax rate decreases as the level of income rises.

*Your Own Answer*_____

Q197

True or False: Charges for government documents purchased from the Government Printing Office are examples of user fees.

*Your Own Answer*_____

Q198

When equals are treated equally tax-wise, is this considered vertical equity or horizontal equity?

*Your Own Answer*_____

Correct Answers

A196

True. This system is easier on the wealthy and tougher on the poor.

A197

True. These are not considered taxes because taxes fall on everyone, while user fees fall only on people especially served by certain government services.

A198

Horizontal equity

Questions

Q199

True or False: The higher the marginal tax rate, the less an individual can keep out of any additional income earned.

*Your Own Answer*_____

Q200

True or False: It is fairly easy to measure the monetary value an individual receives from national defense.

*Your Own Answer*_____

Q201

People should pay taxes based on their income or their wealth. Is this idea called the benefit principle or the ability-to-pay principle?

*Your Own Answer*_____

Correct Answers

A199

True. The more income one makes, the higher the federal income tax bracket he or she is in. This means that richer people earning more money pay more proportionally to the government in taxes and keep the rest.

A200

False. We all benefit the national defense, but it is hard to place a monetary value on this benefit.

A201

Ability-to-pay principle

Questions

Q202

True or False: A good tax is one that does not adversely affect the decisions to work, save, and invest.

*Your Own Answer*_____

Q203

True or False: The higher the marginal tax rate, the more an individual can keep of any additional income earned.

*Your Own Answer*_____

Q204

If marginal tax rates are too high, will this lead individuals in these high tax brackets to work harder or to work less?

*Your Own Answer*_____

Correct Answers

A202

True. Taxes are mainly to raise money for the government and are not supposed to affect how individuals handle their money, for the most part.

A203

False. An individual with a higher marginal tax rate, say 38%, can keep only 62% (100% − 38% = 62%) of the additional income earned.

A204

To work less. They won't think it is desirable to work harder when the government receives such a high percentage of their extra income.

Questions

Q205

True or False: If people save and invest less, this will tend to lower the standard of living of the society.

*Your Own Answer*_____

_____

Q206

True or False: Economists generally favor the complicated income tax over the simple income tax.

*Your Own Answer*_____

_____

Q207

True or False: Not all taxpayers can afford the benefits they receive from the government.

*Your Own Answer*_____

_____

Correct Answers

A205

True. Investing leads to more jobs and more productivity. Less investing decreases the number of jobs and the amount of work done.

A206

False. Tax systems that are easier to understand and to comply with are preferred.

A207

True. Welfare recipients pay few taxes yet receive benefits of welfare that they can't pay for.

Questions

Q208

An individual should pay taxes according to the amount of money or services he will receive from the government. Is this statement concerning the ability-to-pay principle or the benefits principle?

*Your Own Answer*_____

_____

Q209

Is the progressive income tax based on the benefits principle or the ability-to-pay principle?

*Your Own Answer*_____

_____

Q210

True or False: The government deficit is the same as the government national debt.

*Your Own Answer*_____

_____

Correct Answers

A208

The benefits principle. According to this principle, if you get more benefits, you should pay more taxes

A209

The ability-to-pay principle. Rich people are able to pay a higher tax rate because they have higher incomes.

A210

False. The deficit is the amount in a year by which the government spending exceeds its income. The total of all the deficits over the years, less the surpluses, if any, is the national debt.

Questions

Q211

True or False: If the government spending in a year is less than its income, the government has a deficit for that year.

*Your Own Answer*_____

Q212

True or False: Over the years the federal government has run more deficits than surpluses.

*Your Own Answer*_____

Q213

True or False: When the government pays its debts by borrowing from another source, this is called refinancing.

*Your Own Answer*_____

Correct Answers

A211

False. If spending is less than income, the government has a surplus for that year.

A212

True. Almost every year there is a government deficit.

A213

True. Usually the government sells more bonds in order to get money to pay off maturing bonds.

Questions

Q214

True or False: A good example of a public good is national defense, because everybody in the country is protected.

*Your Own Answer*_____

_____

Q215

True or False: A private good is rival, because the consumption of the good (like eating bread) reduces the amount available for all others.

*Your Own Answer*_____

_____

Q216

A non-exclusion means that non-taxpayers cannot be prevented from using the item. Is an example of a non-exclusion a city park or a bottle of soda pop?

*Your Own Answer*_____

_____

Correct Answers

A214

True. Whether a person pays taxes or not, he or she is protected by the military.

A215

True. If we eat the bread, there may not be any more left for others.

A216

City park. Even people paying little or no taxes can sit on a city park bench.

Questions

Q217

True or False: The government can compel people to pay taxes.

*Your Own Answer*_____

Q218

Are items that the government supplies, like public television, considered by economists to be merit goods and services, or are they externalities?

*Your Own Answer*_____

Q219

True or False: An example of an externality is government regulation of pollution.

*Your Own Answer*_____

Correct Answers

A217

True. People who don't pay real estate taxes have their homes taken away from them.

A218

Merit goods and services. The government provides them because it thinks they are in the best interests of the public.

A219

True. An externality is when a market transaction between two parties affects a third party.

Questions

Q220

True or False: Economic conservatives favor pure market economy.

*Your Own Answer*_____

Q221

True or False: Economic conservatives agree with the ability-to-pay theory of taxation.

*Your Own Answer*_____

Q222

Do economic conservatives believe that the government should participate in the economy actively or that participation should be quite limited?

*Your Own Answer*_____

Correct Answers

A220

True. They believe the less government interference in the economy the better.

A221

False. These conservatives believe in the benefit theory.

A222

Quite limited. They want less government.

Questions

Q223

True or False: Economic conservatives believe that government is inherently efficient and that its actions are usually equitable.

*Your Own Answer*_____

_____

Q224

True or False: Economic conservatives believe that inflation and recession are largely caused by mismanaged fiscal and monetary policies.

*Your Own Answer*_____

_____

Q225

True or False: Economic liberals believe that widespread monopoly and consumer and worker ignorance lead to market inefficiency.

*Your Own Answer*_____

_____

Correct Answers

A223

False. They believe government is inefficient and that its actions are frequently inequitable.

A224

True. Government mismanagement is the major cause of these problems in their opinion.

A225

True. Liberals don't blame government for these problems, but they do blame monopolies.

Questions

Q226

The distribution of income and wealth is distorted by economic power and discrimination. Is this a liberal or a conservative view?

*Your Own Answer*_____

_____

Q227

True or False: Economic conservatives believe there needs to be widespread government participation in the economy to protect consumers and workers, and to distribute income fairly.

*Your Own Answer*_____

_____

Q228

Major economic problems are the result of too little government oversight, not too much oversight. Is this a liberal or a conservative economic view?

*Your Own Answer*_____

_____

Correct Answers

A226

Liberal. Liberals blame business power and dis-crimination.

A227

False. This is a liberal viewpoint.

A228

Liberal

Questions

Q229

True or False: The gross national product is a measurement of society's well being.

*Your Own Answer*_____

Q230

True or False: A measure of the dollar value of final goods and services produced by the economy over a given period of time, usually a year, is called gross national product.

*Your Own Answer*_____

Q231

Does cost of goods sold less cost of intermediate goods purchased equal gross national product, or does it equal value added?

*Your Own Answer*_____

Correct Answers

A229

False. It is an economic measure, not a social measure.

A230

True

A231

Value added

Questions

Q232

True or False: The market value equals the market price of the good or service times the quantity.

*Your Own Answer*_____

_____

Q233

True or False: If the current year's market price of goods or services is used in the computation, do we get nominal gross national product or real gross national product?

*Your Own Answer*_____

_____

Q234

Is another name for nominal gross national product called real gross national product, or is it called current dollar gross national product?

*Your Own Answer*_____

_____

Correct Answers

A232

True

A233

Nominal gross national product

A234

Current dollar gross national product. Nominal gross national product, also called current dollar gross national product, is usually only for one year and doesn't take inflation into consideration. On the other hand, real gross national product has been recomputed to take inflation into consideration.

Questions

Q235

True or False: Another name for real gross national product is constant dollar gross national product.

*Your Own Answer*_____

Q236

True or False: The use of real gross national product facilitates comparisons of gross national product across the years.

*Your Own Answer*_____

Q237

True or False: A base year is an arbitrarily chosen year which is used as the basis of comparison in an analysis.

*Your Own Answer*_____

Correct Answers

A235

True. Both of these mean the same thing and are computed by taking inflation into consideration.

A236

True. This is so because the inflation factor is taken out of it.

A237

True. A base year must be used in the computation to change nominal gross national product to real gross national product.

Questions

Q238

True or False: The gross national product deflator is usually given as a percentage and is a measure of the average price level in a given year.

*Your Own Answer*_____

Q239

True or False: The gross national product deflator for the base year is always given the value of 100.

*Your Own Answer*_____

Q240

True or False: If the deflator was 108 in the year after the base year, the average level of prices would have risen by 4%.

*Your Own Answer*_____

Correct Answers

A238

True. It is used to compare prices among various years.

A239

True. Any year can be picked as the base year, but it is always then given the value of 100.

A240

False. It would have risen by 8%.

Questions

Q241

True or False: Criminal activity is included in gross national product computations.

Your Own Answer

Q242

True or False: Sales of used cars are included in the measurement of gross national product.

Your Own Answer

Q243

True or False: Gross national product includes national and personal assets.

Your Own Answer

Correct Answers

A241

False. Only those goods and services that have been sold in markets are included.

A242

False. Only newly-produced items are included.

A243

False. Gross national product includes goods and services that the economy produces in a year, not the value of assets already accumulated.

Questions

Q244

True or False: Gross national product would include the value of burglar alarms produced in the year.

*Your Own Answer*_____

Q245

True or False: Gross national product would include the value of leisure time in a society.

*Your Own Answer*_____

Q246

True or False: Gross national product and gross national income add up to the same figure in any one year.

*Your Own Answer*_____

Correct Answers

A244

True. This is production.

A245

False. It includes only the dollar value of the production of goods and services.

A246

True. They mean the same thing in the long run.

Questions

Q247

True or False: The imputed value of owner-occupied housing is part of the gross national product.

*Your Own Answer*_____

Q248

True or False: Government spending for goods and services is included in gross national product.

*Your Own Answer*_____

Q249

True or False: Capital goods "wear down" with use or time. Depreciation is an estimate of this reduction in value and is a cost of production.

*Your Own Answer*_____

Correct Answers

A247

True. This is one of the few examples of non-market production in the gross national product.

A248

True. This is part of gross national product.

A249

True

Questions

Q250

True or False: Gross national product less capital consumption allowances—also called capital depreciation—give net national product.

*Your Own Answer*_____

Q251

True or False: Net national product is a widely-used measure for economists.

*Your Own Answer*_____

Q252

Is disposable income what households have to save or spend as they please?

*Your Own Answer*_____

Correct Answers

A250

True

A251

False. Net national product is not widely used.

A252

Yes. This is what they have left to save or spend after taxes have been paid.

Questions

Q253

Are business cycles more noticeable in a planned economy or in a market-oriented economy?

*Your Own Answer*_____

_____

Q254

True or False: People without a job who are not actively seeking a job are considered unemployed.

*Your Own Answer*_____

_____

Q255

True or False: The labor force consists of all people who have a job but does not include people actively seeking a job.

*Your Own Answer*_____

_____

Correct Answers

A253

In a market-oriented economy. These alternating periods of prosperity and recession are characteristic of a free economy.

A254

False. They must be without a job and actively seeking a job.

A255

False. The labor force includes all people who have a job plus all people who are actively seeking a job.

Questions

Q256

True or False: Most economists believe that full employment is obtained when the unemployment rate is in the 4% to 5.5% range.

*Your Own Answer*_____

_____

Q257

Are workers who are "in between jobs" considered to be part of structural unemployment or frictional unemployment?

*Your Own Answer*_____

_____

Q258

True or False: Discouraged people who want a job but have given up looking for a job are counted in the labor force.

*Your Own Answer*_____

_____

Correct Answers

A256

True. This is the place where the number of vacant jobs is just equal to the number of unemployed people.

A257

Frictional unemployment. Structurally unemployed people are those who lack the skills needed to fill available job openings.

A258

False. They must be actively seeking work to be counted in the labor force.

Questions

Q259

True or False: Disinflation is the same as deflation.

*Your Own Answer*_____

Q260

Is a period of time when both unemployment and inflation are high called hyperinflation or stag-flation?

*Your Own Answer*_____

Q261

True or False: A "market basket of goods and ser-vices" is used by the government in computing the consumer price index.

*Your Own Answer*_____

Correct Answers

A259

False. Deflation is a sustained, substantial decrease in the average level of prices, while disinflation is a decrease in the rate of inflation.

A260

Stagflation. Hyperinflation is a period of extremely rapid inflation and has nothing to do with employment levels.

A261

True. This market basket is usually given an index number of 100 for the base year.

Questions

Q262

True or False: The consumer price index is an extremely refined measure of the cost of living.

*Your Own Answer*_____

Q263

True or False: The "market basket" used in computing the consumer price index is continually altered to take into account the introduction of new products.

*Your Own Answer*_____

Q264

Will people who hold large sums of cash in the bank be better off or worse off during the times of inflation?

*Your Own Answer*_____

Correct Answers

A262

False. The index is only a rough measure of the cost of living. It is for a "typical family" and no real family is "typical."

A263

False. New products are not taken into account each year.

A264

Worse off. During times of high inflation, the value of money in terms of purchasing power drops drastically.

Questions

Q265

True or False: If consumers prefer a product, the demand curve will shift inward.

*Your Own Answer*_____

_____

Q266

True or False: If consumers prefer a product, the equilibrium price will decrease.

*Your Own Answer*_____

_____

Q267

True or False: If consumers prefer more of a product, the equilibrium quantity will increase.

*Your Own Answer*_____

_____

Correct Answers

A265

False. The demand curve will shift outward on the chart to show increased demand.

A266

False. The equilibrium price will increase because if supply stays the same but demand increases, this will tend to increase the price.

A267

True. If there is more demand, there will have to be more production in order to achieve equilibrium.

Questions

Q268

True or False: Let us say a depression occurs and consumers begin to prefer a product less. On the chart, the demand curve will move out.

*Your Own Answer*_____

Q269

True or False: If consumers prefer less of a product, such as fewer men preferring felt hats, the equilibrium price will decrease.

*Your Own Answer*_____

Q270

True or False: As people's income increases, they desire to buy more luxury goods like filet mignon.

*Your Own Answer*_____

Correct Answers

A268

False. The demand curve will move in, showing less demand.

A269

True. A lower demand will lower the equilibrium price.

A270

True. Richer people enjoy and are more able to afford luxuries as their incomes increase.

Questions

Q271

True or False: As people's income increases, the equilibrium price of the luxury goods they wish to buy increases.

*Your Own Answer*_____

Q272

True or False: As people's income increases, their desire to buy filet mignon or other luxury goods causes the demand curve to shift inward.

*Your Own Answer*_____

Q273

True or False: Margarine is considered a normal good.

*Your Own Answer*_____

Correct Answers

A271

True. The people have both the desire and the ability to buy these luxury goods, so the equilibrium price increases.

A272

False. This desire causes the demand curve to shift outward.

A273

False. Margarine is considered an inferior good. As people earn more income, they buy less margarine and more butter.

Questions

Q274

True or False: Butter is considered an inferior good.

Your Own Answer

Q275

True or False: As people become richer and their incomes increase, their desire and tendency to buy butter causes the demand curve to remain the same.

Your Own Answer

Q276

True or False: As people's income increases, their demand for margarine causes the demand curve to shift inward.

Your Own Answer

Correct Answers

A274

False. Butter is considered a normal good because as people earn more income, they tend to buy more butter.

A275

False. It causes the demand curve to shift outward.

A276

True. They demand less margarine causing an inward shift.

Questions

Q277

True or False: A depression occurs and people have lower incomes. This causes the demand curve for margarine to shift inward.

*Your Own Answer*_____

_____

Q278

True or False: Let us say that times get better and people's income increases. This will tend to cause a decrease in the equilibrium price of margarine.

*Your Own Answer*_____

_____

Q279

True or False: People are richer. The equilibrium price of margarine increases.

*Your Own Answer*_____

_____

Correct Answers

A277

False. They have less money so they make due with margarine instead of buying butter.

A278

True. Margarine is an inferior good, and better times cause people to buy more butter and less margarine. This causes the equilibrium price of margarine to decrease.

A279

False. Richer people buy less margarine, so the equilibrium price of margarine drops.

Questions

Q280

True or False: When times are bad and people's incomes drop, the equilibrium price of margarine increases.

*Your Own Answer*_____

Q281

True or False: When people's incomes drop, the equilibrium quantity of margarine produced also drops.

*Your Own Answer*_____

Q282

True or False: If the price of a substitute good, such as brown bread, increases, how does this affect the demand curve for white bread? It makes the curve for white bread shift out.

*Your Own Answer*_____

Correct Answers

A280

True. People with lower incomes buy less butter and more margarine.

A281

False. People buy less butter and more margarine and their incomes drop, so that equilibrium quantity of margarine produced increases.

A282

True. If the price of brown bread increases, the demand curve for white bread will move outward on the chart because there will be more demand for white bread.

Questions

Q283

True or False: If the price of a substitute good—such as brown bread—increases, the price of white bread will be affected.

*Your Own Answer*_____

Q284

True or False: If the price of a substitute good—such as brown bread—increases, the equilibrium quantity of white bread will increase.

*Your Own Answer*_____

Q285

True or False: The price of tennis racquets increases. How will this affect the demand curve for tennis balls? The demand curve for tennis balls will increase.

*Your Own Answer*_____

Correct Answers

A283

False. The price of white bread will also increase because people have switched from brown bread to white bread, causing an increase in the demand for white bread.

A284

True. White bread is a substitute for brown bread, so the quantity of white bread produced will also increase, forcing the equilibrium quantity to increase.

A285

False. An increase in the price of tennis racquets will cut the quantity of tennis racquets sold. Since people will buy fewer tennis racquets they will also buy fewer tennis balls, causing the demand curve for tennis balls to be less and to shift inward.

Questions

Q286

True or False: The price of tennis racquets increases. How will this affect the equilibrium price for tennis balls? The equilibrium price for tennis balls will decrease.

*Your Own Answer*_____

Q287

True or False: The price of tennis racquets increases. How will this affect the equilibrium quantity of tennis balls produced? It will increase the equilibrium quantity of tennis balls produced.

*Your Own Answer*_____

Q288

True or False: Let us say that the price of tennis racquets decreases. How will this affect the demand curve for tennis balls? It will cause the demand curve for tennis balls to shift outward.

*Your Own Answer*_____

Correct Answers

A286

True. There will be less demand for racquets, so there will be less demand for tennis balls, which will cause the equilibrium price for tennis balls to decrease.

A287

False. It will decrease the equilibrium quantity of tennis balls produced. There will be less demand for tennis racquets and this will translate into less demand for tennis balls also.

A288

True. The price of racquets decreases, causing more demand for racquets. This will also cause more demand for tennis balls, causing the demand curve to shift outward.

Questions

Q289

True or False: Let us say that the price of tennis racquets decreases. How will this affect the equilibrium price for tennis balls? It will cause the equilibrium price of tennis balls to increase, all other things being equal.

*Your Own Answer*_____

Q290

True or False: Let us say that the price of tennis racquets is decreasing. How will this affect the equilibrium quantity of tennis balls? It will cause the equilibrium quantity of tennis balls to decrease.

*Your Own Answer*_____

Q291

True or False: Let us say a war comes and the government expects that we will soon have price inflation. This will cause the demand curve to shift inward.

*Your Own Answer*_____

Correct Answers

A289

True. The decreasing price of tennis racquets will cause more demand for tennis racquets. The increasing demand for tennis racquets will cause an increasing demand for tennis balls, causing the equilibrium price of tennis balls to increase.

A290

False. It will cause the equilibrium quantity of tennis balls to increase because the lower price of racquets causes more of a demand for tennis balls. The greater demand for tennis balls will cause the equilibrium quantity for tennis balls to increase.

A291

False. The demand curve will shift outward because war brings prosperity and increased demand.

Questions

Q292

True or False: Let us say that a war begins and the government expects prices to rise. This will cause the equilibrium price to increase.

*Your Own Answer*_____

Q293

True or False: Let us say that there is no war, but the nation is experiencing increased prosperity. Prices are expected to rise, and the equilibrium quantity will also rise.

*Your Own Answer*_____

Q294

True or False: Let us say that the nation is heading into a downward swing in the economy and the government expects prices to fall. This will cause the demand curve to shift outward.

*Your Own Answer*_____

Correct Answers

A292

True. A price increase causes an equilibrium price increase.

A293

True. A rise in prices means that demand exceeds supply, so industry will start increasing the supply, which will increase the equilibrium quantity.

A294

False. The demand curve will shift inward because poorer times usually mean decreasing demand.

Questions

Q295

True or False: The nation moves into a recession and the price level is expected to fall. The equilibrium price will also fall.

*Your Own Answer*_____

Q296

True or False: The nation is moving toward a recession and the government expects the price level to fall. This will also cause a decrease in the equilibrium quantity amount.

*Your Own Answer*_____

Q297

True or False: Let us say that the cost of raw materials is increasing. This will cause the supply curve to shift outward.

*Your Own Answer*_____

Correct Answers

A295

True. If prices generally fall, the equilibrium price level also drops.

A296

True. As prices fall, there is less demand for production, so the equilibrium quantity will fall to meet the lower demand level.

A297

False. It will cause the supply curve to shift inward, because the higher cost of raw materials will cut demand.

Questions

Q298

True or False: Let us say that raw material prices are increasing. This will cause an increase in equilibrium price.

*Your Own Answer*_____

Q299

True or False: The raw material prices are increasing. This will also cause an increase in equilibrium quantity.

*Your Own Answer*_____

Q300

True or False: Let us say that the cost of raw materials is decreasing. This will push the supply curve outward.

*Your Own Answer*_____

Correct Answers

A298

True. The raw material price increase will cause an increase in the price of finished goods, thus also pushing the equilibrium price upward.

A299

False. As raw material prices increase, it will cause an increase in the price of finished goods, which will result in a lower demand. This lower demand will cause a decrease in the equilibrium quantity.

A300

True. A decrease in the cost of raw materials should cause a greater demand for the products so that more of the products will be produced, thus causing the supply curve to move outward.

Questions

Q301

True or False: The cost of raw materials is decreasing. This should cause a decrease in the equilibrium price.

*Your Own Answer*_____

Q302

True or False: Let us say that technology advances. For instance, we might be able to buy faster, smaller, and cheaper calculators. This will result in the supply curve to shift inward.

*Your Own Answer*_____

Q303

True or False: Let us say that the new calculators are faster and cheaper. This will cause the equilibrium price to decrease also.

*Your Own Answer*_____

Correct Answers

A301

True. As cost prices decrease, this should also cause the prices of finished goods to decrease, which would make the equilibrium price decrease also.

A302

False. The new, faster, and cheaper calculators will have a high demand. This will cause an increase in production, so the supply curve would shift outward.

A303

True. As retail prices for the calculators fall, the equilibrium price of the calculators will also fall.

Questions

Q304

True or False: Technology advances, and faster and cheaper calculators are being produced. The equilibrium quantity will decrease.

*Your Own Answer*_____

_____

Q305

True or False: Let us say a war comes and all production goes toward war products, and peace technology, such as the production of new calculators, retreats. The supply curve for new calculators will shift inward.

*Your Own Answer*_____

_____

Q306

True or False: Let us say a war comes and all production goes toward war products, and peace technology, such as the production of new calculators, retreats. The equilibrium price will decrease.

*Your Own Answer*_____

_____

Correct Answers

A304

False. The big demand for the new calculators will cause an increase in production. This will cause an increase in the equilibrium quantity.

A305

True. There will be a small production of calculators per year, and this will cause the supply curve to shift inward.

A306

False. The war will cause a small supply of calculators, but there will be increased demand. In the absence of price controls, this will cause the price of calculators to increase, so the equilibrium price will also increase.

Questions

Q307

True or False: Let us say a war comes and all production goes towards war products, and peace technology, such as the production of new calculators, retreats. The equilibrium quantity will also decrease.

*Your Own Answer*_____

Q308

True or False: Let us say that war comes to our nation. Factories making calculators are bombed and many calculators are destroyed. This will result in causing the supply curve to shift inward.

*Your Own Answer*_____

Q309

True or False: Let us say that war comes to our nation. Factories making calculators are bombed and many calculators are destroyed. This will result in a decrease in the equilibrium price of calculators.

*Your Own Answer*_____

Correct Answers

A307

True. A decrease in production will carry over to a decrease in equilibrium quantity.

A308

True. The bombing will cause a lower supply of calculators, and the supply curve will shift inward.

A309

False. The supply of calculators has dropped because of the bombing, yet there is a high demand for calculators. If there are no price controls, the price of calculators will increase, and this will also cause the equilibrium price of calculators to increase.

Questions

Q310

True or False: Let us say that war comes to our nation. Factories making calculators are bombed and many calculators are destroyed. This will cause a decrease in the equilibrium quantity of calculators.

*Your Own Answer*_____

Q311

True or False: The nation's economy is improving, and the government expects the price of calculators to rise. The supply curve will shift inward.

*Your Own Answer*_____

Q312

True or False: The nation's economy is improving, and the government expects the price of calculators to rise. The equilibrium price will increase.

*Your Own Answer*_____

Correct Answers

A310

True. A decrease in the number of calculators on the market will also cause a decrease in the equilibrium quantity.

A311

True. All else being equal, if prices rise, there will be less demand for the product. The lower demand will cause the manufacturers to produce fewer calculators, and this will cause the supply curve to move inward.

A312

True. As the price of calculators rises, so does the equilibrium price.

Questions

Q313

True or False: The nation's economy is improving, and the government expects the price of calculators to rise. The equilibrium quantity will increase.

*Your Own Answer*_____

Q314

True or False: The nation seems to be moving into a recession. Prices of calculators, along with prices of all products, are expected to fall. The supply curve will shift inward.

*Your Own Answer*_____

Q315

True or False: If Say's Law is true, a general glut of unsold goods on the market will never occur.

*Your Own Answer*_____

Correct Answers

A313

False. The equilibrium quantity will decrease. All else being equal, if prices rise, there will be less demand for the product. The lower demand will cause the manufacturers to produce fewer calculators, so the equilibrium quantity will decrease.

A314

False. As prices fall, people will buy more calculators. This will cause an increase in the production of calculators, so the supply curve will shift outward.

A315

True. Say believed that supply creates its own demand, and that all the products produced will be purchased.

Questions

Q316

True or False: If, at a certain time, people don't save much and there isn't much money to be lent out, yet a great number of people wish to borrow money, this will cause the interest rates to drop.

*Your Own Answer*_____

_____

Q317

True or False: If there is a glut in merchandise on the shelves of stores, economists believe this can be solved by lowering prices.

*Your Own Answer*_____

_____

Q318

True or False: Today, most economists consider themselves Keynesians.

*Your Own Answer*_____

_____

Correct Answers

A316

False. The supply is less than the demand, so interest rates should rise.

A317

True. Low prices will cause people to buy more goods.

A318

True. Keynes believed in government intervention in economic policy, and this is what most economists believe today.

Questions

Q319

True or False: Keynes believed that wages seldom fall.

Your Own Answer_____

_____

Q320

Some economists believe that the interest rate is a strong determinant of either saving or investment. Is this idea Keynesian or is it classical in economics?

Your Own Answer_____

_____

Q321

In the absence of appropriate government policy, instability will be the hallmark of a capitalistic economy. Is this idea Keynesian or is it classical?

Your Own Answer_____

_____

Correct Answers

A319

True. Wages rise in response to market conditions, but they seldom fall.

A320

Classical. Classical economists believe the interest rate change will keep saving and investment equal. This idea is not shared by Keynesian economists.

A321

Keynesian. Keynes believed that governmental interference is necessary in order to keep a stable economy.

Questions

Q322

True or False: Saving without investing, according to Keynes, will cause an increase of production and employment.

*Your Own Answer*_____

Q323

True or False: According to Keynes, if government suspects too little spending will be forthcoming in the economy, it could increase its own spending or else reduce taxes so that the private sector can spend more.

*Your Own Answer*_____

Q324

True or False: Keynes wrote his book, *The General Theory of Employment, Interest, and Money* during prosperous times.

*Your Own Answer*_____

Correct Answers

A322

False. It will contract the economy causing less production and less employment.

A323

True. This action on the part of the government will keep the economy in full swing, according to Keynes.

A324

False. He wrote during worldwide depression.

Questions

Q325

True or False: Keynes agrees with Say's Law.

*Your Own Answer*_____

Q326

True or False: Households can spend more than they earn over a short period of time by drawing down on assets.

*Your Own Answer*_____

Q327

Does the annual profit divided by investment give the dollar value of the annual return or does it give the rate of return?

*Your Own Answer*_____

Correct Answers

A325

False. Say's Law states that demand creates its own supply, but Keynes thinks that government must often step in to increase demand.

A326

True. If a household spends more than it saves, it will have to use some of its assets to pay its bills.

A327

Rate of return. The dollar value of the annual return is the same as annual profit.

Questions

Q328

True or False: The marginal efficiency of investment is the rate of return on the first dollar invested.

*Your Own Answer*_____

_____

Q329

True or False: When the prices of foreign goods and services fall relative to domestic goods and services, more foreign goods and services will be demanded.

*Your Own Answer*_____

_____

Q330

True or False: A closed, private economy is one with no international trade and no government.

*Your Own Answer*_____

_____

Correct Answers

A328

False. It is the rate of return on the last dollar invested.

A329

True. People will buy the cheaper, foreign-made goods.

A330

True. There is no such thing in real life as a closed economy, but economists use closed economy models to get across certain theories.

Questions

Q331

Does aggregate expenditure equal investment, or does aggregate expenditure equal investment plus consumption?

*Your Own Answer*_____

Q332

True or False: If aggregate expenditure is greater than gross national product, then current production is insufficient to satisfy demand. Firms may be forced to draw down on their inventories.

*Your Own Answer*_____

Q333

True or False: If, in a year, national income is greater than national spending, then current production exceeds demand, and the economy will contract.

*Your Own Answer*_____

Correct Answers

A331

Investment plus consumption. Aggregate means total, so the total expenditure of the economy for a year would include both investment and consumption. Of course, if consumption is as high as aggregate expenditure, there would be no money left for investment.

A332

True. People are willing and able to buy more than is produced that year.

A333

False. People have more income than they need, so current production is insufficient to satisfy demand, and the economy will expand.

Questions

Q334

True or False: If, over the year, inventories increase, current production will exceed demand and the excess will be placed in inventory leading firms to reduce production.

*Your Own Answer*_____

Q335

Additional spending raises income which leads to additional spending which raises income still more, which leads to further spending which raises income, and so on. Is this idea known to economists as the Equilibrium Principle or the Multiplier Principle?

*Your Own Answer*_____

Q336

True or False: Spending has a multiplier effect as its results filter through the economy. Economists also believe that investment has a multiplier effect.

*Your Own Answer*_____

Correct Answers

A334

True. Larger inventories mean that production is greater than sales, so this will lead to less production in the future.

A335

Multiplier Principle. Increased spending multiplies as its results filter through the economy.

A336

True. If a dollar comes from outside the economy and into the nation's economy, its effects will multiply as it goes through the economy.

Questions

Q337

Is the amount of output that the economy is capable of producing at full employment called the gross national product, or is it called the potential gross national product?

*Your Own Answer*_____

Q338

According to Keynes, will insufficient spending in the nation lead the economy to an equilibrium above or below the potential gross national product?

*Your Own Answer*_____

Q339

Does Keynes think recessions are caused by too much investment or by too little spending?

*Your Own Answer*_____

Correct Answers

A337

Potential gross national product. It is the economy's output if full employment level could be attained.

A338

Below. There isn't as much spending as there should be, so the equilibrium is below what it should be.

A339

By too little spending. It is spending that keeps the wheels of the economy running.

Questions

Q340

According to Keynes, will too much spending lead the economy to an equilibrium below or above the potential gross national product?

*Your Own Answer*_____

Q341

True or False: Keynes believed that the economy is not capable of producing more than its potential for extended periods of time.

*Your Own Answer*_____

Q342

True or False: If there is too much spending as compared with production, it will lead the economy to an equilibrium below the potential gross national product.

*Your Own Answer*_____

Correct Answers

A340

Above. Spending fuels the economy, and too much of it pushes the equilibrium too high.

A341

True. The economy can only produce so much per year.

A342

False. It will lead the economy to an equilibrium above potential gross national product. Spending will be greater than production.

Questions

Q343

According to Keynes, is inflation caused by too much production or by too much spending?

Your Own Answer_____

Q344

Will increased government spending multiply as it travels through the economy?

Your Own Answer_____

Q345

True or False: Increased taxes reduce the gross national product as much as four times the amount of the tax increase.

Your Own Answer_____

Correct Answers

A343

By too much spending. At any one time the spending is greater than production. This causes too much money to chase too few goods, thus resulting in inflation.

A344

Yes, it will multiply up to five times.

A345

True. This is known as the tax multiplier.

Questions

Q346

True or False: If government spending is increased $1 and taxes are increased $1, the total effect on gross national product will be zero.

*Your Own Answer*_____

Q347

Are changes in government spending and taxes consciously made by the government to achieve certain stabilization goals referred to as automatic stabilizers, or are they referred to as discretionary fiscal policy?

*Your Own Answer*_____

Q348

True or False: A good example of discretionary fiscal policy would be that if the economy threatens to head into a recession, the government would make a decision to increase taxes.

*Your Own Answer*_____

Correct Answers

A346

False. The net effect will be positive because government spending has a stronger stimulative effect
than taxes have a dampening effect.

A347

Discretionary fiscal policy

A348

False. In order to head off a recession, the government should decrease taxes, thus leaving more
money in the hands of the people.

Questions

Q349

True or False: A good example of discretionary fiscal policy would be that if the economy threatens to head into a recession, the government would make a decision to increase its spending.

*Your Own Answer*_____

Q350

True or False: A good example of discretionary fiscal policy would be that if the economy threatens to head into a recession, the government would make a decision to decrease taxes.

*Your Own Answer*_____

Q351

True or False: A good example of discretionary fiscal policy would be that if the economy threatens to head into a recession, the government would decrease its spending.

*Your Own Answer*_____

Correct Answers

A349

True. Increased government spending, through the government spending multiplier, would flow through the economy and lift it by about five times the actual government spending increase, thus helping to ward off the recession.

A350

True. A decrease in taxes would leave more money in the hands of the public, and they would use much of this extra money to buy goods, thus checking the slide into recession.

A351

False. A decrease in government spending would cut down the economy throughout the system, and with reverse multiplier effect, would add to the slide toward recession.

Questions

Q352

True or False: When unemployment goes up, government spending for unemployment compensation increases. This is an example of discretionary fiscal policy.

*Your Own Answer*_____

Q353

True or False: When the economy falls into recession, personal income tax collections by the government increase in dollar value.

*Your Own Answer*_____

Q354

True or False: During periods of full employment, government spending for unemployment compensation decreases.

*Your Own Answer*_____

Correct Answers

A352

False. It is an example of one of the government's automatic stabilizers. Unemployment compensation payments by the government increase automatically when unemployment increases and the unemployed apply for this aid.

A353

False. Personal income tax collections fall during recessions as wages drop and people lose their jobs.

A354

True. Few people apply for unemployment compensation at this time.

Questions

Q355

During periods of full employment, government spending for unemployment compensation decreases. Is this an example of government discretionary fiscal policy or is it an example of an automatic stabilizer?

*Your Own Answer*_____

Q356

True or False: Inflation dangers are the greatest during recessions.

*Your Own Answer*_____

Q357

True or False: As a rule, automatic stabilizers cannot cure recession or inflation, but make the problem less severe than it otherwise would be.

*Your Own Answer*_____

Correct Answers

A355

Automatic stabilizer. Fewer people apply for unemployment compensation, so it is automatic.

A356

False. Inflation dangers are greatest during times of full or near-full employment.

A357

True. These automatic stabilizers help, but they are usually not enough by themselves to cure either inflation or recession.

Questions

Q358

True or False: The government fiscal year begins on July 1.

*Your Own Answer*_____

Q359

True or False: Deciding on a proper budget to meet the stabilization needs of the economy requires the ability to forecast accurately more than one year into the future, something that economists are usually quite good at doing.

*Your Own Answer*_____

Q360

True or False: An estimate of what government spending, taxes, and the deficit would be if the economy were at full employment is called structural budget.

*Your Own Answer*_____

Correct Answers

A358

False. It begins on October 1 each year.

A359

False. Economics is a social science, and all economists don't agree with each other. Most of them are good at looking backward but not so good at looking forward.

A360

True. It is also called full employment budget.

Questions

Q361

True or False: By estimating spending, taxes, and the deficit at full employment, economists remove the effect of the economy on the budget.

*Your Own Answer*_____

_____

Q362

True or False: Many economists believe that the government should run a deficit during recessions.

*Your Own Answer*_____

_____

Q363

True or False: Many economists believe that the government should run a surplus during inflationary times.

*Your Own Answer*_____

_____

Correct Answers

A361

True. As the economy changes, the automatic stabilizers keep changing the government's actual income and spending. This budget at full employment takes the effects of the economy out of the budget.

A362

True. A deficit means that government spending is higher than government taxes. Through the multiplier effect, this helps recovery.

A363

True. A surplus is caused by the government spending less than it takes in. This would tend to slow the economy down and minimize inflation.

Questions

Q364

True or False: The government deficit is the same thing as the government debt.

*Your Own Answer*_____

Q365

True or False: In a household, a $20,000 debt is more burdensome to a household earning $50,000 per year than one earning $200,000.

*Your Own Answer*_____

Q366

True or False: The burden of debt to an entity can only be properly assessed by comparing it to the entity's financial condition.

*Your Own Answer*_____

Correct Answers

A364

False. The deficit is a yearly figure which is the difference between government income and government expenses. Each year's deficit increases the government debt by the amount of the deficit. Conversely, a government surplus would decrease the government debt by the amount of the surplus.

A365

True. Families with big incomes usually have more discretionary funds with which to pay off debts.

A366

True. If the entity is making plenty of money, it can pay off its debts much easier than if it is not making money.

Questions

Q367

The government borrows from other sources to pay back the creditors whose loans have become due. Is this known as refinancing the debt or distributing the debt?

*Your Own Answer*_____

_____

Q368

When an institution is unable to pay its debts, is this known as deficit or bankruptcy?

*Your Own Answer*_____

_____

Q369

If the government can't pay its debts, it can simply print money. Is this a liberal or conservative point of view?

*Your Own Answer*_____

_____

Correct Answers

A367

Refinancing the debt

A368

Bankruptcy

A369

Liberal. Most conservatives want the government to pay off the debt through either increased taxes or decreased spending. Printing money leads to inflation, which is the worst type of unfair tax, according to conservatives.

Questions

Q370

When the deficit is large and the government has to borrow a great deal of money, does this tend to decrease or increase the interest rate?

*Your Own Answer*_____

_____

Q371

True or False: Inflation is more likely when the economy is operating well below potential than it is if the economy is at or near full employment.

*Your Own Answer*_____

_____

Q372

True or False: Money is the most liquid of all assets.

*Your Own Answer*_____

_____

Correct Answers

A370

Increase the interest rate. Demand for money is higher than the supply of money, so the interest rate increases.

A371

False. Inflation is more likely to occur when the economy is at or near full potential.

A372

True. Liquidity refers to the ease with which an asset can be transferred into spendable form. Money is already in spendable form.

Questions

Q373

True or False: Money usually pays a lower return than do other assets.

*Your Own Answer*_____

Q374

True or False: Money has to have intrinsic value.

*Your Own Answer*_____

Q375

Are traveler's checks considered M1 or M2?

*Your Own Answer*_____

Correct Answers

A373

True. Money in the bank, even in a savings account, usually pays less than money invested in real estate or stocks or bonds.

A374

False. Gold coins have intrinsic value because the gold in them has a value in itself. However, paper money is worth something because the government backs it up, even though it does not have any value in itself as paper.

A375

M1

Questions

Q376

True or False: Checking accounts in a bank are considered M2.

*Your Own Answer*_____

Q377

True or False: Savings accounts in a bank are considered M1.

*Your Own Answer*_____

Q378

True or False: Reserves are liabilities on a bank's balance sheet.

*Your Own Answer*_____

Correct Answers

A376

True. They are both M1 and M2.

A377

False. They are M2.

A378

False. They are assets because they are cash or demand deposits held in other banks. The bank needs to pay its depositors or pay off checks drawn on the bank.

Questions

Q379

True or False: Loans are assets on a bank's balance sheet.

*Your Own Answer*_____

Q380

True or False: Savings deposits are assets on the bank's balance sheet.

*Your Own Answer*_____

Q381

True or False: The required reserve ratio is set for the banks by Congress.

*Your Own Answer*_____

Correct Answers

A379

True. They are similar to accounts receivable.

A380

False. The bank owes this money to depositors, so it is a liability similar to accounts payable.

A381

False. It is set by the Federal Reserve System.

Questions

Q382

True or False: Excess reserves are the difference between the amount of reserves a bank holds and what it is required to hold.

*Your Own Answer*_____

Q383

True or False: Banks hold enough reserves on hand to honor the demands of all depositors, even if all depositors tried to withdraw their money simultaneously.

*Your Own Answer*_____

Q384

True or False: Fractional reserve banking means that banks hold enough reserves to pay depositors, even if all depositors desired to withdraw their money at the same time.

*Your Own Answer*_____

Correct Answers

A382

True

A383

False. If all depositors tried to withdraw their money simultaneously, banks would not be able to honor the demands.

A384

False. Fractional reserve banking means banks constantly operate holding reserves that are only a part of their deposit liabilities.

Questions

Q385

True or False: In banking, excess reserves earn a return for the bank.

*Your Own Answer*_____

Q386

True or False: When banks lend out their excess reserves, this increases the nation's money supply.

*Your Own Answer*_____

Q387

True or False: Banks often lend out more than the amount of their excess reserves.

*Your Own Answer*_____

Correct Answers

A385

False. Excess reserves are extra money that a bank is holding in its vaults. This money has not been lent out, so it is not earning interest.

A386

True. Usually, this money is spent quickly by the borrower and it is then placed in another bank. This increases demand deposits, which are part of the nation's money supply.

A387

False. The banks must keep their required reserves on hand.

Questions

Q388

True or False: If the required reserve ratio is 20%, then the deposit expansion multiplier is 5.

*Your Own Answer*_____

Q389

True or False: If the required reserve ratio is 25%, then the deposit expansion multiplier is 4.

*Your Own Answer*_____

Q390

True or False: Multiple expansion of the money supply is a product of the action of the one bank lending the money, and not of all banks in the banking system.

*Your Own Answer*_____

Correct Answers

A388

True. It is the reciprocal.

A389

True. It is the reciprocal.

A390

False. It is the product of all banks in the banking system. No one bank lends out more than its excess reserves.

Questions

Q391

True or False: Every bank holds some excess reserves.

Your Own Answer

Q392

True or False: Some of the new money created by bank loans leaks out into cash and is not redeposited in a bank.

Your Own Answer

Q393

True or False: There is no central bank of the United States.

Your Own Answer

Correct Answers

A391

True. Banks keep some extra cash on hand at all times, more than the Federal Reserve System requires, to lend to prospective customers.

A392

True. Most people put money back into the safekeeping of some bank, but some people save money and carry it around with them or put it into jars or in a mattress.

A393

False. The central bank is known as the Federal Reserve System.

Questions

Q394

True or False: Part of the Federal Reserve System's job is to conduct monetary policy to fight inflation and unemployment and to stimulate economic growth.

*Your Own Answer*_____

Q395

Is the Federal Reserve System owned by the federal government or by member banks?

*Your Own Answer*_____

Q396

True or False: The Fed can be considered an independent agency of the federal government.

*Your Own Answer*_____

Correct Answers

A394

True. The Fed performs these and other monetary functions.

A395

It is nominally owned by member banks. The power of banks to own the Fed was given by the Federal Reserve Act of 1913.

A396

True. It runs itself but must report to Congress.

Questions

Q397

True or False: The Federal Reserve System's Board of Directors is directly accountable to the people.

*Your Own Answer*_____

Q398

True or False: Congress approves or disapproves bank mergers.

*Your Own Answer*_____

Q399

When depositors lose faith in their bank and try to withdraw their money, is this called bank regulations or is it called bank panic?

*Your Own Answer*_____

Correct Answers

A397

False. The Board is appointed by the President and confirmed by the Senate, but their terms last 14 years, so they are virtually independent.

A398

False. The Federal Reserve System does this.

A399

Bank panic. It's also called a run on a bank.

Questions

Q400

True or False: The Federal Reserve System helps reduce bank panics by being a lender of last resort.

*Your Own Answer*_____

Q401

True or False: The Federal Deposit Insurance provides government guarantees for bank deposits should a bank fail.

*Your Own Answer*_____

Q402

True or False: The Federal Reserve System is allowed by the government to engage in open market operations.

*Your Own Answer*_____

Correct Answers

A400

True. People know that the Federal Reserve System will back up banks in trouble, so this prevents panics.

A401

True. When banks fail, this government agency steps in to bail them out up to certain limits.

A402

True. This is one of the ways the Fed controls the money supply.

Questions

Q403

If the Federal Reserve System wishes to expand the money supply, would they buy bonds in the open market, or would they sell bonds in the open market?

*Your Own Answer*_____

_____

Q404

What would the Federal Reserve System probably desire to do during times of recession?

*Your Own Answer*_____

_____

Q405

If the Federal Reserve System sold bonds in the open market, would this tend to increase the money supply or decrease the money supply?

*Your Own Answer*_____

_____

Correct Answers

A403

They would buy bonds in the open market. The Fed would use money to pay for these bonds, and this money would flow through the financial system, greatly increasing the money supply.

A404

Lower interest rates. During times of recession, lower interest rates would cause more borrowing and investing, thus tending to end the recession.

A405

Decrease the money supply. Money would come into the Federal Reserve Banks from the purchasers of the bonds, so there would be less money in circulation and the money supply would be decreased.

Questions

Q406

Would the Federal Reserve System wish to decrease the money supply during times of depression or during times of inflation?

*Your Own Answer*_____

Q407

If the Federal Reserve System wishes to cut inflation, should it lower interest rates, or should it raise interest rates?

*Your Own Answer*_____

Q408

True or False: There is usually no secondary market for bonds.

*Your Own Answer*_____

Correct Answers

A406

During times of inflation. Inflation is too much money chasing too few goods, causing increases in prices. To stop too much money being in circulation, the Fed could sell bonds on the open market, thus causing less money to be in circulation and thus holding down inflation.

A407

It should raise interest rates. This will make money harder for individuals and businesses to borrow, so there will be less money, thus reducing inflation.

A408

False. If a bondholder wishes to sell his bond prior to its maturity date, this can usually be done by selling the bond in the so-called "secondary market."

Questions

Q409

True or False: There is an inverse relationship between bond yield and bond price.

*Your Own Answer*_____

Q410

If banks are deficient in reserves, they will have to call in loans and stop making loans to potential customers. Will this cause interest rates to rise or fall?

*Your Own Answer*_____

Q411

If the Federal Reserve System raises the legal reserve ration for the banks, will this tend to increase or decrease the member banks' ability to lend money?

*Your Own Answer*_____

Correct Answers

A409

True. As the bond price rises, the yield percentage falls and vice versa.

A410

Interest rates will rise. The demand for loans will be greater than the supply of money, so interest rates will go up.

A411

Decrease. The member banks will have to keep more of their funds in reserve, so they won't be able to lend out so much money.

Questions

Q412

If the Federal Reserve Bank reduces the reserve requirements, will this tend to contract the economy or expand the economy?

*Your Own Answer*_____

Q413

In order to contract the economy, would the Federal Reserve System raise the discount rate or would it lower the discount rate?

*Your Own Answer*_____

Q414

True or False: A household's demand for money is positively related to its income.

*Your Own Answer*_____

Correct Answers

A412

Expand the economy. The member banks will not need to keep so much money on reserve, so they will have more money to lend out to businesses and to individuals. This extra money in circulation will tend to expand the economy.

A413

Raise the discount rate. This would make it more difficult to borrow and thus would contract the amount of money in circulation.

A414

True. Households with higher incomes spend more money and, therefore, need to hold more money to finance those transactions.

Questions

Q415

True or False: A household's demand for money is negatively related to the interest rate.

*Your Own Answer*_____

Q416

True or False: Money in cash form typically pays no or very low interest.

*Your Own Answer*_____

Q417

If we multiply the one dollar income by the number of times it changes hands, we get the amount of income created. Is this known as the quantity theory of money, or is it known as the equation of exchange?

*Your Own Answer*_____

Correct Answers

A415

True. If the interest rate rises, the household will probably keep less of its assets in the form of money, because they could acquire more interest by investing it elsewhere.

A416

True. Money in cash form in your pocket pays no interest. Cash in the bank pays no or very low interest.

A417

Equation of exchange. If you multiply the money supply by the rate at which money changes hands, you get the level of income.

Questions

Q418

Is the rate at which money changes hands known as the quantity theory of money, or is it known as the velocity of money?

*Your Own Answer*_____

_____

Q419

The price level is determined by the quantity of money. Is this the quantity theory of money, or is it modern monetarism?

*Your Own Answer*_____

_____

Q420

Changes in the money supply are the most important factor affecting the economy. Is this a belief of classical economists or modern monetarists?

*Your Own Answer*_____

_____

Correct Answers

A418

Velocity of money

A419

Quantity theory of money. This is what classical economists believed in early days.

A420

Modern monetarists. They believe a surplus of money, or a dearth of money, is the main thing affecting the economy.

Questions

Q421

True or False: Modern monetarists believe that the Federal Reserve System should use discretionary monetary policy in an attempt to stabilize the economy.

*Your Own Answer*_____

Q422

True or False: As a rule, economists are very good at forecasting what the economy will do in the next year.

*Your Own Answer*_____

Q423

True or False: Modern monetarists believe the Federal Reserve System should let the money supply grow at a constant rate.

*Your Own Answer*_____

Correct Answers

A421

False. They believe that the Federal Reserve System should NOT use discretionary monetary policy in an attempt to stabilize the economy.

A422

False. Unfortunately, but truthfully, economists are not very apt at forecasting the economy.

A423

True. As the population grows, the money supply should grow. This should smooth out the economic curve.

Questions

Q424

If the level of spending in the economy exceeds production, is this demand pull inflation, or is it cost push inflation?

*Your Own Answer*_____

Q425

True or False: According to Keynes, inflation is unlikely to occur when the economy is operating below the full-employment level.

*Your Own Answer*_____

Q426

If the economy has high unemployment and high inflation at the same time, is this called cost push inflation, or is it called stagflation?

*Your Own Answer*_____

Correct Answers

A424

Demand pull inflation

A425

True. At this level, increased demand will cause increased hiring of unemployed resources, causing more output.

A426

Stagflation. Prices are going up, yet costs increase forcing firms to lay off employees.

Questions

Q427

True or False: When labor unions win demands for excessive wages, forcing their employers to raise their prices, this is called stagflation.

*Your Own Answer*_____

Q428

Which of the following will eventually cut inflation—raising the money supply or raising taxes?

*Your Own Answer*_____

Q429

Does supply-side economics favor increased output, or does it favor tax cuts?

*Your Own Answer*_____

Correct Answers

A427

False. It is called cost push inflation. The union's demands for higher wages have raised the costs of production, thus pushing up sales prices.

A428

Raising taxes will cause the public to have less discretionary money to spend and will cut inflation. Raising the money supply, on the other hand, will tend to increase inflation.

A429

Tax cuts. Fewer taxes mean that people will have more money to save and invest.

Questions

Q430

True or False: Supply-side economists believe that tax rate cuts will increase government revenues.

*Your Own Answer*_____

Q431

Looking at international trade, the gains to a nation from specializing and trading exceed the losses. This theory would be valid in discussing which one—comparative advantage or absolute advantage?

*Your Own Answer*_____

Q432

Is a tax applied on an imported good called a tariff or a quota?

*Your Own Answer*_____

Correct Answers

A430

True. They believe that marginal tax rates are so high that people won't work as hard as they otherwise might. They think that cuts in marginal tax rates will stimulate production and actually increase government revenues.

A431

Comparative advantage. In absolute advantage, only one of the two countries can produce the product, like bananas. In discussing specialization, both countries can produce the product, so we are discussing comparative advantage.

A432

A tariff. A quota is a limitation on the amount of goods that can be imported.

Questions

Q433

True or False: When individuals with different circumstances pay different amounts of tax, this is considered vertical equity.

*Your Own Answer*_____

Q434

Resources are limited and desires are unlimited. This is _____, the basic problem of economics.

*Your Own Answer*_____

Q435

A businessman doubles the inputs used in his production process. As a result, his output triples. This is an example of _____ .

*Your Own Answer*_____

Correct Answers

A433

True. Vertical equity is achieved when unequals are treated unequally.

A434

scarcity

A435

increasing returns to scale

Questions

Q436

A good that is used in the production of another good is a _____.

*Your Own Answer*_____

Q437

True or False: The wealthier the nation, the more remote the production possibility curve is from the origin.

*Your Own Answer*_____

Q438

True or False: Economics as a science is said to have started with the publication of *Wealth of Nations* in 1776.

*Your Own Answer*_____

Correct Answers

A436

capital good

A437

True

A438

True

Questions

Q439

True or False: Economics as a science differs from the "natural" sciences because the economist cannot perform controlled experiments.

Your Own Answer

Q440

A bond which can be redeemed before maturity at the discretion of its issuer is a(n) _____ bond.

Your Own Answer

Q441

A bond which can be exchanged for common stock at a previously specified ratio is a(n) _____.

Your Own Answer

Correct Answers

A439

True

A440

callable

A441

convertible bond

Questions

Q442

The _____ is the dominant form of business organization in terms of number of firms, but the _____ is the dominant form in terms of output.

*Your Own Answer*_____

Q443

A(n) _____ is the term given to any item of wealth owned by a firm or individual.

*Your Own Answer*_____

Q444

The legal responsibility of a stockholder for the debt of a corporation up to the amount of his investment only is called _____.

*Your Own Answer*_____

Correct Answers

A442

single proprietorship; corporation

A443

asset

A444

limited liability

Questions

Q445

True or False: One principal reason for the formation of a corporation is the greater ease corporations have in obtaining funds.

*Your Own Answer*_____

Q446

True or False: In order to begin operations, a corporation must obtain a state charter.

*Your Own Answer*_____

Q447

True or False: Because they represent a fixed payment, bonds are a greater burden on a firm than stocks during a period in which receipts are low.

*Your Own Answer*_____

Correct Answers

A445

True

A446

True

A447

True

Questions

Q448

True or False: In comparison with stocks, bonds offer a limited, but steady income.

*Your Own Answer*_____

Q449

GNP per capita, in _____ dollars, can be used as the measure of the standard of living because it ignores inflation and deflation.

*Your Own Answer*_____

Q450

The total income earned in any given year by resource suppliers is measured by _____.

*Your Own Answer*_____

Correct Answers

A448

True

A449

constant

A450

national income

Questions

Q451

True or False: According to classical theory, an increase in the desire to save will lower the interest rate and, in so doing, will increase investment by a corresponding amount.

*Your Own Answer*_____

Q452

The partial freezing of federal construction expenditures during the Vietnam inflation is an example of _____ fiscal policy.

*Your Own Answer*_____

Q453

A federal tax levied on a domestically produced commodity is called a(n) _____.

*Your Own Answer*_____

Correct Answers

A451

True

A452

discretionary

A453

excise tax

Questions

Q454

The largest single source of the federal government's tax revenue is the _____.

*Your Own Answer*_____

Q455

Legal tax avoidance that lets income go untaxed or be taxed at a lower level is called _____.

*Your Own Answer*_____

Q456

An income tax with _____ rates causes after-tax income to be more equally distributed than before-tax income.

*Your Own Answer*_____

Correct Answers

A454

personal income tax

A455

tax loopholes

A456

progressive

Questions

Q457

The fact that dividends are taxed as both corporate income and personal income is referred to as ____.

*Your Own Answer*_____

Q458

The tax which is imposed on a product at each stage of production is called the ____.

*Your Own Answer*_____

Q459

True or False: The federal income tax is the only major tax on individuals in the U.S. that is progressive.

*Your Own Answer*_____

Correct Answers

A457

double taxation

A458

value added tax

A459

True

Questions

Q460

True or False: In a progressive tax structure, marginal tax rate is always greater than or equal to average tax rate.

*Your Own Answer*_____

Q461

In forecasting the economic future, models build up constant estimates of spending based upon _____ patterns.

*Your Own Answer*_____

Q462

Inflation benefits _____ at the expense of creditors.

*Your Own Answer*_____

Correct Answers

A460

True

A461

past

A462

debtors

Questions

Q463

True or False: Every mixed economy has the knowledge to create whatever domestic purchasing power it needs for full employment.

*Your Own Answer*_____

_____

Q464

True or False: There can be no inflation without an increase in the money supply.

*Your Own Answer*_____

_____

Q465

True or False: Money must be kept relatively scarce in order to maintain its value.

*Your Own Answer*_____

_____

Correct Answers

A463

True

A464

False

A465

True

Questions

Q466

True or False: Money is anything that is widely accepted as a medium of exchange.

*Your Own Answer*_____

_____

Q467

The fraction of deposits that the Federal Reserve requires commercial banks to keep in vault cash or balances at the Fed is called _____.

*Your Own Answer*_____

_____

Q468

In balance sheet terms, a bank's deposits are _____.

*Your Own Answer*_____

_____

Correct Answers

A466

True

A467

the required reserve ratio

A468

liabilities

Questions

Q469

The _____ is the governmental agency responsible for safe-guarding all bank deposits.

*Your Own Answer*_____

Q470

The principle assets of banks are their _____ .

*Your Own Answer*_____

Q471

True or False: A commercial bank may lend out all of its excess reserves.

*Your Own Answer*_____

Correct Answers

A469

Federal Deposit Insurance Corporation

A470

loans

A471

True

Questions

Q472

True or False: Commercial banks have the power to print money.

*Your Own Answer*_____

Q473

True or False: New loans made by commercial banks increase the money supply.

*Your Own Answer*_____

Q474

The _____ can be thought of as the price of borrowing money.

*Your Own Answer*_____

Correct Answers

A472

False

A473

True

A474

interest rate

Questions

True or False: Twenty years ago, the dollar would buy roughly twice what it buys now.

*Your Own Answer*_____

The discount rate is always _____ the market interest rate.

*Your Own Answer*_____

The reduction in the discount rate ultimately has _____ as its purpose.

*Your Own Answer*_____

Correct Answers

A475

True

A476

less than

A477

economic expansion

Questions

Q478

The _____ banks are required to be members of the Federal Reserve System.

*Your Own Answer*_____

Q479

True or False: The U.S. Federal Reserve System consists of a central Federal Reserve Board and twelve regional Federal Reserve Banks.

*Your Own Answer*_____

Q480

True or False: The Federal Reserve's major function is to control the national money supply.

*Your Own Answer*_____

Correct Answers

A478

national

A479

True

A480

True

Questions

Q481

True or False: Open market operations are performed by the Fed approximately once a month.

*Your Own Answer*_____

_____

Q482

The relationship between the price of a commodity and the quantity of it offered for sale is called _____.

*Your Own Answer*_____

_____

Q483

The relationship between the price of a commodity and the quantity buyers are willing and able to purchase is called _____.

*Your Own Answer*_____

_____

Correct Answers

A481

False. While they are not performed monthly, they are performed several times throughout the year.

A482

supply

A483

demand

Questions

Q484

Cameras and film are _____ goods.

*Your Own Answer*_____

Q485

True or False: The higher the legal minimum wage is set, the more jobs will be available for the unskilled.

*Your Own Answer*_____

Q486

True or False: A supply curve shifting to the right means that producers will supply more at each price.

*Your Own Answer*_____

Correct Answers

A484

complementary

A485

False

A486

True

Questions

Q487

If two goods are _____ , the higher price of one of them is likely to have an adverse effect on the demand for both goods.

*Your Own Answer*_____

Q488

The more substitutes for a given good are readily available, the more _____ its demand curve is likely to be.

*Your Own Answer*_____

Q489

True or False: Utility is a psychological concept and, therefore, cannot be precisely measured.

*Your Own Answer*_____

Correct Answers

A487

complements

A488

elastic

A489

True

Questions

Q490

Supply curves tend to be more elastic in the _____ run.

*Your Own Answer*_____

_____

Q491

A horizontal line is used to draw a(n) _____ demand.

*Your Own Answer*_____

_____

Q492

Wages, fuel, and raw materials are examples of _____ costs.

*Your Own Answer*_____

_____

Correct Answers

A490

long

A491

perfectly elastic

A492

variable

Questions

Q493

Costs that are incurred regardless of the level of production are called _____.

*Your Own Answer*_____

Q494

_____ at any output level is the extra cost incurred by producing one additional unit of output.

*Your Own Answer*_____

Q495

The point where total revenue is equal to total cost is called the _____ point.

*Your Own Answer*_____

Correct Answers

A493

fixed

A494

Marginal cost

A495

break-even

Questions

Monopolies for which it would be impractical for producers to compete are called ＿＿＿ .

Your Own Answer _____

The practice of firms in an industry following the price changes initiated by members of the industry is called ＿＿＿ .

Your Own Answer _____

True or False: Despite changing birth rates and technology, labor's relative share of national product has dropped over the decades.

Your Own Answer _____

Correct Answers

A496

natural monopolies

A497

price leadership

A498

False

Questions

Q499

By the _____ we mean the ratio of the export prices to the import prices.

*Your Own Answer*_____

Q500

_____ quotas are designed to persuade foreigners to place limits on their exports to the U.S.

*Your Own Answer*_____

Q501

The _____ modified the Wagner Act, chiefly, by citing unfair labor union practices.

*Your Own Answer*_____

Correct Answers

A499

terms of trade

A500

Voluntary

A501

Taft-Hartley Act

Questions

Q502

_____ clauses gear wages to changes in the cost of living.

Your Own Answer_____

Q503

Under a _____ agreement, one must belong to the union before being hired.

Your Own Answer_____

Q504

The _____ established the National Labor Relations Board.

Your Own Answer_____

Correct Answers

A502

Escalator

A503

closed shop

A504

Wagner Act

Questions

Q505

The economic system in which the government owns and operates the basic industries is called _____.

*Your Own Answer*_____

Q506

The economy system of the U.S. is sometimes referred to as a _____.

*Your Own Answer*_____

Q507

True or False: Adam Smith was an earnest defender of laissez-faire policy because he believed the capitalist economy to be self-regulatory.

*Your Own Answer*_____

Correct Answers

A505

socialism

A506

mixed economy

A507

True

Questions

Q508

True or False: *Wealth of Nations* shows the division of labor and capital accumulation to be the major means of economic expansion and growth.

*Your Own Answer*_____

_____

Q509

If a firm like IBM controls 80% of the market, this is an example of a _____ monopoly.

*Your Own Answer*_____

_____

Q510

The individual supply curve for labor starts by rising, but slopes _____ after a point.

*Your Own Answer*_____

_____

Correct Answers

A508

True

A509

near

A510

backward

Questions

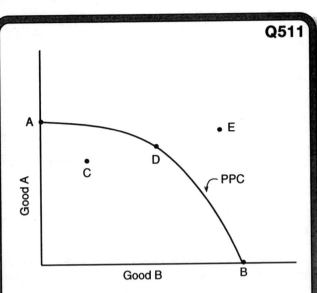

Q511

Production Possibilities Frontier Curve

a) Using the figure above for the Production Possibilities Frontier Curve, what point represents the maximum of Good A that could be produced if all resources were directed for production of Good A?

b) Using the figure above for the Production Possibilities Frontier Curve, what point represents the maximum of Good B that could be produced if all resources were directed for production of Good B?

c) If the company does not use its full resources, its production point could be at which point?

d) When could production be at Point E?

Your Own Answers _____

_____

_____

Correct Answers

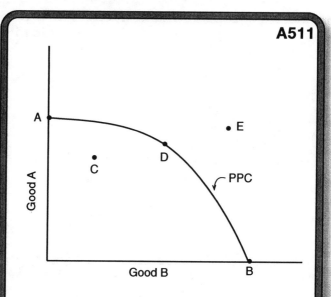

Production Possibilities Frontier Curve

a) Point A

b) Point B

c) Point C

d) Never

Questions

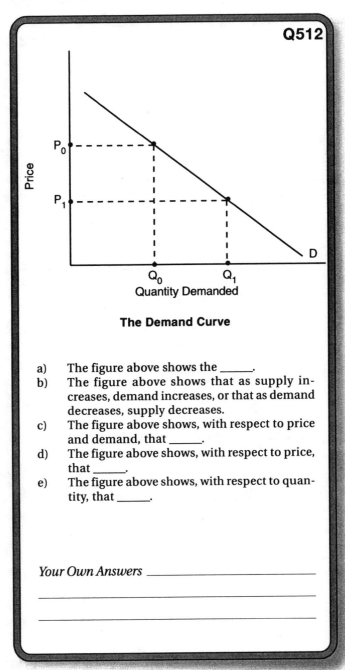

The Demand Curve

a) The figure above shows the _____.

b) The figure above shows that as supply increases, demand increases, or that as demand decreases, supply decreases.

c) The figure above shows, with respect to price and demand, that _____.

d) The figure above shows, with respect to price, that _____.

e) The figure above shows, with respect to quantity, that _____.

Your Own Answers _____

_____

_____

Correct Answers

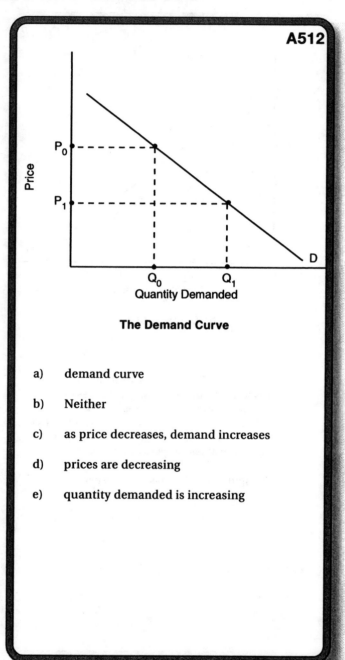

The Demand Curve

a) demand curve

b) Neither

c) as price decreases, demand increases

d) prices are decreasing

e) quantity demanded is increasing

Questions

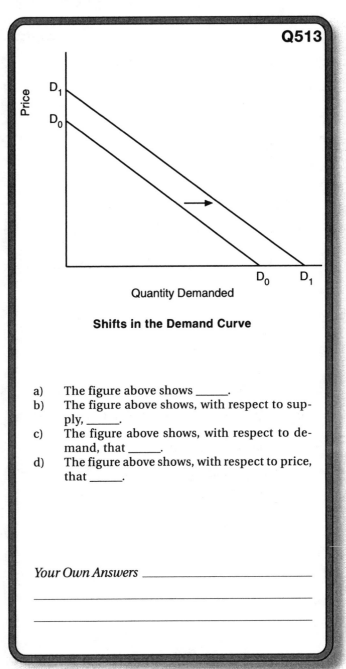

Q513

Price

D₁
D₀

Quantity Demanded

D₀   D₁

Shifts in the Demand Curve

a)   The figure above shows _____.
b)   The figure above shows, with respect to sup-
     ply, _____.
c)   The figure above shows, with respect to de-
     mand, that _____.
d)   The figure above shows, with respect to price,
     that _____.

Your Own Answers _____

_____

_____

Correct Answers

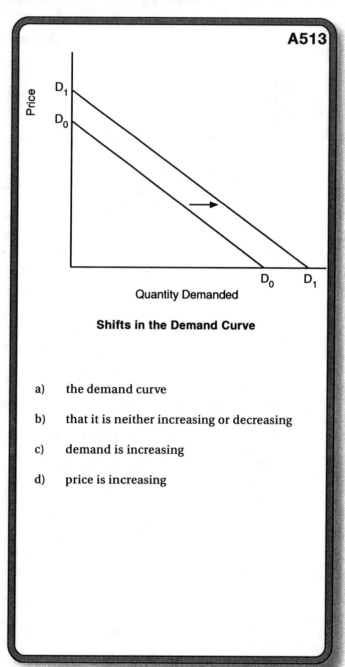

A513

Shifts in the Demand Curve

a)   the demand curve

b)   that it is neither increasing or decreasing

c)   demand is increasing

d)   price is increasing

Questions

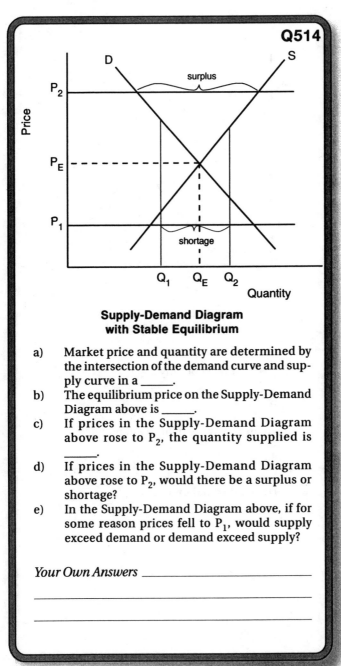

Q514

**Supply-Demand Diagram
with Stable Equilibrium**

a) Market price and quantity are determined by
    the intersection of the demand curve and sup-
    ply curve in a _____.

b) The equilibrium price on the Supply-Demand
    Diagram above is _____.

c) If prices in the Supply-Demand Diagram
    above rose to P_2, the quantity supplied is

    _____.

d) If prices in the Supply-Demand Diagram
    above rose to P_2, would there be a surplus or
    shortage?

e) In the Supply-Demand Diagram above, if for
    some reason prices fell to P_1, would supply
    exceed demand or demand exceed supply?

Your Own Answers _____

_____

_____

Correct Answers

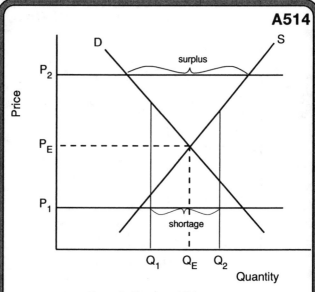

A514

**Supply-Demand Diagram
with Stable Equilibrium**

a)   free market economy

b)   E

c)   greater than the quantity demanded

d)   Surplus

e)   Demand would exceed supply.

Questions

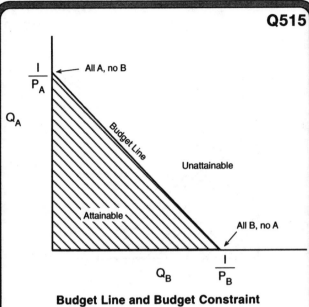

Budget Line and Budget Constraint

a) **True or False:** In the above figure, the first quantity is called Q_A and the second quantity is called Q_B.

b) **True or False:** The Budget Line in the figure above shows all obtainable combinations of two baskets of goods.

c) Why is the shaded part of the figure called "Attainable"?

d) Why is the unshaded part of the figure called "Unattainable"?

e) In the above figure, is the Budget Line positive or negative?

f) **True or False:** The above figure shows the feasible rate that one can trade off A for B.

Your Own Answers _____

_____

_____

Correct Answers

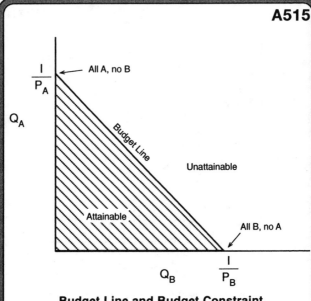

Budget Line and Budget Constraint

a) True. Quantity A is higher on the chart and is read first.

b) True. Runs from A to B.

c) Because it is within the budget constraints

d) Because it is beyond the budget constraints

e) Negative

f) True. A and B are substitutes for each other.

Questions

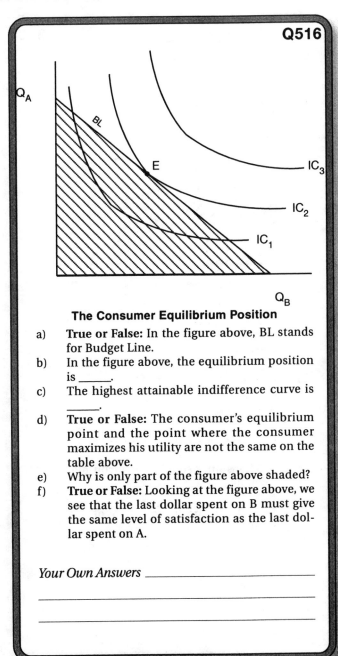

The Consumer Equilibrium Position

a) **True or False:** In the figure above, BL stands for Budget Line.

b) In the figure above, the equilibrium position is _____.

c) The highest attainable indifference curve is _____.

d) **True or False:** The consumer's equilibrium point and the point where the consumer maximizes his utility are not the same on the table above.

e) Why is only part of the figure above shaded?

f) **True or False:** Looking at the figure above, we see that the last dollar spent on B must give the same level of satisfaction as the last dollar spent on A.

Your Own Answers _____

_____

_____

Correct Answers

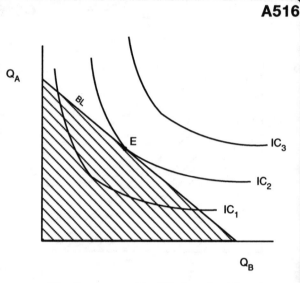

The Consumer Equilibrium Position

a) True. Budget Line shows limited funds available.

b) E

c) IC_1

d) False. They are both at point E.

e) The consumer should not spend more than his budget.

f) True. This is true due to the Law of Equal Marginal Utility.

Questions

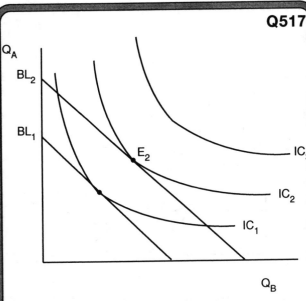

Shifts in Budget Line on Equilibrium Position

a) What is meant by indifference curve?

b) **True or False:** The figure above shows that as income decreases, the budget line will shift to the left.

c) **True or False:** The figure above shows that a proportional decrease in the price of both Quantity A and Quantity B will shift the budget line to the right.

Your Own Answers _____

_____

_____

Correct Answers

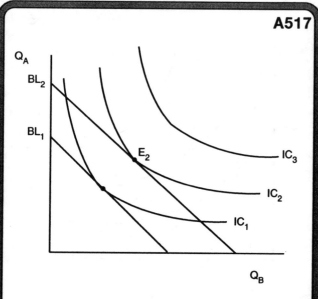

Shifts in Budget Line on Equilibrium Position

a) At the middle of the curve the consumer will not care which product he or she buys.

b) True. Chart makeup.

c) True. A decrease in prices leaves the consumer with more money thus more budget to spend on something else.

Questions

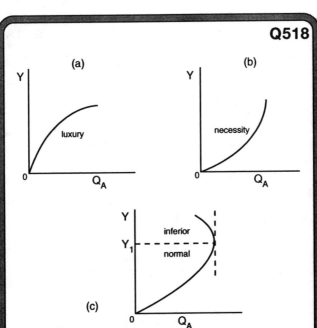

The Engel Curve and the Categories of Goods

a) What does Engle Curve (a) figure mean?
b) What does Engle Curve (b) figure mean?
c) **True or False:** What does Engle Curve (c) fig-
    ure mean? Engle Curve (c) figure shows that
    the good is inferior between 0 and Y_1, and that
    the good is normal above Y_1.

Your Own Answers _____

_____

_____

Correct Answers

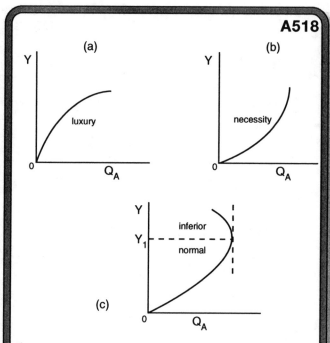

The Engel Curve and the Categories of Goods

a) As a person becomes wealthier, he or she somewhat increases his or her purchases of luxuries, but as the person becomes even more wealthy, his or her purchases of luxuries greatly increase.

b) As a person becomes wealthier, he or she buys fewer necessities proportionately.

c) False. Good is normal between 0 and Y_1 and inferior above Y_1.

Questions

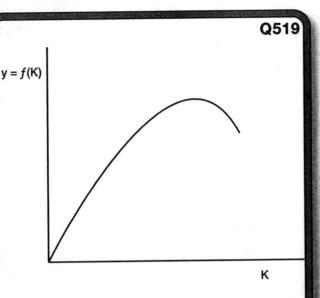

Production Function

a)   **True or False:** The above Production Function
      graph is for one input.
b)   **True or False:** The above Production Function
      graph shows that output is increasing at a de-
      creasing rate.
c)   **True or False:** The above Production Function
      graph shows that when output keeps increas-
      ing, it eventually falls as the input increases.
d)   The above Production Function graph shows
      a diminishing or increasing returns to scale.

Your Own Answers _____

_____

_____

Correct Answers

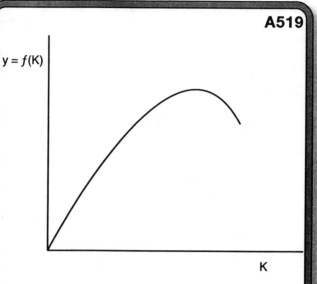

A519

$y = f(K)$

K

Production Function

a)   True. This is the type of chart it is.

b)   True

c)   True. Too much input will not proportionately increase output.

d)   diminishing returns to scale

Questions

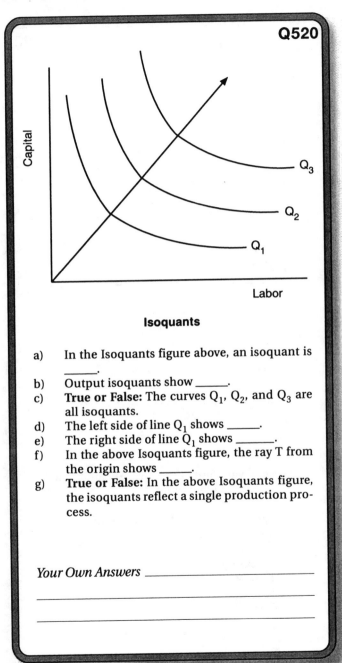

Isoquants

a) In the Isoquants figure above, an isoquant is
_____.

b) Output isoquants show _____.

c) **True or False:** The curves Q_1, Q_2, and Q_3 are all isoquants.

d) The left side of line Q_1 shows _____.

e) The right side of line Q_1 shows _____.

f) In the above Isoquants figure, the ray T from the origin shows _____.

g) **True or False:** In the above Isoquants figure, the isoquants reflect a single production process.

Your Own Answers _____

_____

_____

Correct Answers

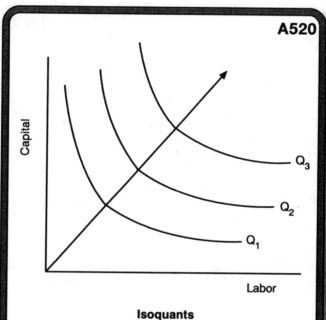

A520

Capital

Q_3

Q_2

Q_1

Label

Labor

Isoquants

a)   a curved line

b)   all the combinations of inputs that will give the same output

c)   True

d)   a great amount of capital input and a smaller amount of labor input

e)   a great amount of labor input and a smaller amount of capital input

f)   increasing output as you move farther from the origin

g)   True

Questions

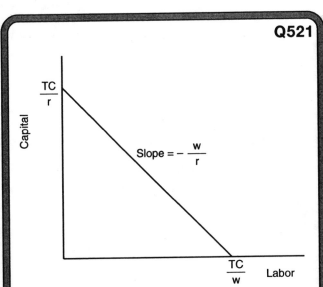

Isocost Curve

a) In the figure above, is the so-called Isocost Curve really a curved or sloped straight line?

b) **True or False:** The Isocost Curve shows different combinations of two given inputs that can be purchased for a certain amount of money.

c) In the figure above, the top left point shows _____.

d) In the figure above, the bottom right point shows _____.

e) In the Isocost figure above, the slanted line has to do with _____.

Your Own Answers _____

_____

_____

Correct Answers

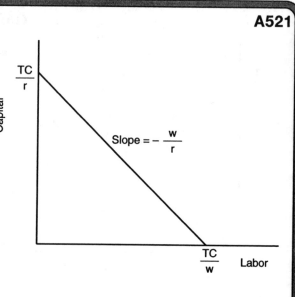

Isocost Curve

a)   A sloped straight line

b)   True. Various amounts of capital and labor.

c)   all capital and no labor

d)   all labor and no capital

e)   cost

Questions

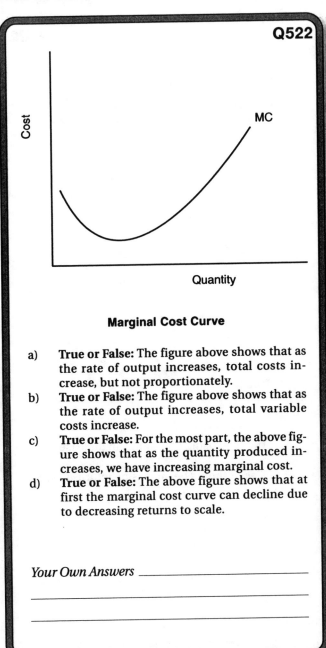

Q522

Marginal Cost Curve

a) **True or False:** The figure above shows that as the rate of output increases, total costs increase, but not proportionately.

b) **True or False:** The figure above shows that as the rate of output increases, total variable costs increase.

c) **True or False:** For the most part, the above figure shows that as the quantity produced increases, we have increasing marginal cost.

d) **True or False:** The above figure shows that at first the marginal cost curve can decline due to decreasing returns to scale.

Your Own Answers _____

_____

_____

Correct Answers

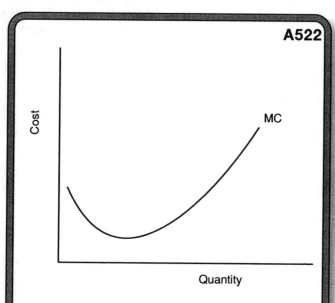

Marginal Cost Curve

a)   True

b)   True

c)   True. The rising line shows an increase.

d)   False. It should be increasing returns to scale.

Questions

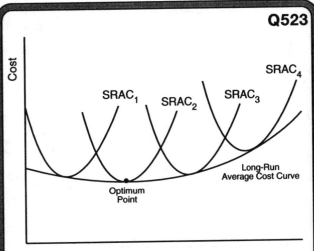

Output Per Time Period

Short-Run Average Cost Curves

a) **True or False:** In the figure above, SRAC stands for Short-Run Average Cost Curve.

b) **True or False:** In the figure above, the long-run average cost curve envelops the short-run average cost curves.

c) **True or False:** The optimum scale of the plant is the point where the short-run average cost curve meets the long-run average cost curve.

d) **True or False:** In the figure above, the long-run average cost curve shows the greatest cost of producing a given level of output.

Your Own Answers _____

_____

_____

Correct Answers

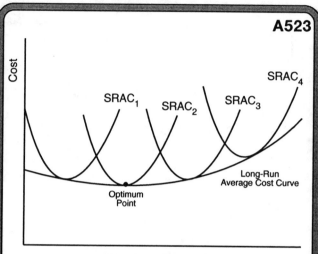

Short-Run Average Cost Curves

a) True

b) True. The figure shows the long-run curve passing by all the short-run curves.

c) True. The long-run average cost curve has a dot on the figure where this is true.

d) False. It shows the least cost.

Questions

Freeze in Florida

a) **True or False:** An unexpected freeze in Florida will increase the supply of orange juice.

b) **True or False:** An unexpected freeze in Florida will increase the price of orange juice.

c) **True or False:** An increase in the price of orange juice will increase the demand for apple juice.

Your Own Answers _____

_____

_____

Correct Answers

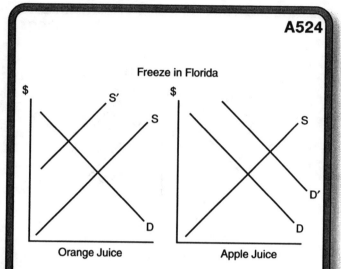

Freeze in Florida

a)   False. Freeze will decrease the supply of oranges.

b)   True. Fewer oranges makes higher prices.

c)   True. Alternative drink.

Questions

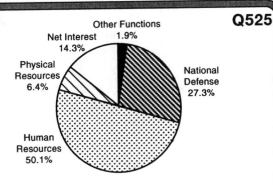

Q525

Federal Expenditures by Category, 1988

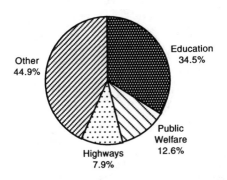

**State and Local Government Spending
by Category, 1988**

a) **True or False:** As of 1988, about 30% of the federal budget went toward net interest payments on the national debt.

b) **True or False:** As of 1988, about 27% of the federal budget was spent for national defense.

c) **True or False:** Almost half of the federal budget goes toward education.

Your Own Answers _____

_____

_____

Correct Answers

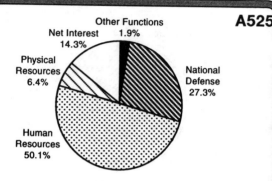

Federal Expenditures by Category, 1988

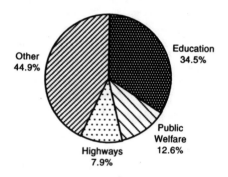

State and Local Government Spending by Category, 1988

a) False. Only about 14%.

b) True. This is the percentage given by government statisticians.

c) False. Education is, for the most part, paid by state and local governments.

Questions

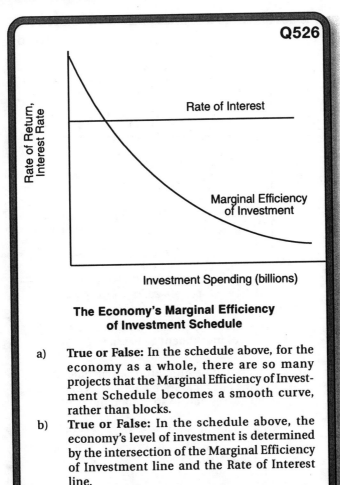

**The Economy's Marginal Efficiency
of Investment Schedule**

a) **True or False:** In the schedule above, for the economy as a whole, there are so many projects that the Marginal Efficiency of Investment Schedule becomes a smooth curve, rather than blocks.

b) **True or False:** In the schedule above, the economy's level of investment is determined by the intersection of the Marginal Efficiency of Investment line and the Rate of Interest line.

c) **True or False:** In the schedule above, everything else being equal, an increase in the tax rate would shift the Marginal Efficiency of Investment line upward and to the right.

Your Own Answers _____

_____

_____

Correct Answers

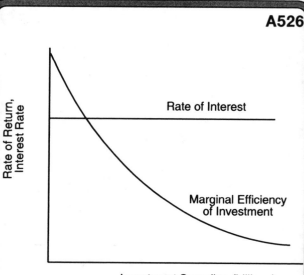

**The Economy's Marginal Efficiency
of Investment Schedule**

a)   True. It will be noted in the schedule above
that the line for Marginal Efficiency of Investment curves downward and to the right.

b)   True. Investment will take place as long as the
marginal efficiency of investment is higher
than the rate of interest.

c)   False. It would shift the line downward and to
the left because the tax rate increase would
mean fewer chances for profitable invest-
ments.

Questions

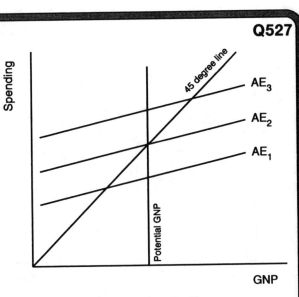

Demand Pull Inflation

a) **True or False:** In the Demand Pull Inflation figure above, line AE_1 is the aggregate level of expenditure at a level below full employment, while line AE_2 is the aggregate level of expenditure at full employment.

b) **True or False:** In the Demand Pull Inflation figure above, an increase in aggregate level of expenditure from line AE_1 to line AE_2 will result in higher gross national product with an increase in the price level.

c) **True or False:** In the Demand Pull Inflation figure above, an increase in aggregate expenditures from line AE_2 to line AE_3 will result in higher gross national product with an increase in the price level.

Your Own Answers _____

_____

_____

Correct Answers

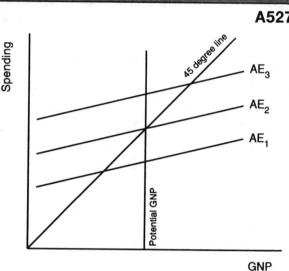

Demand Pull Inflation

a) True. In this case, the line AE_2 shows full employment.

b) False. Although aggregate expenditure increases, line AE_1 is below full employment, so there will be no increase in the price level.

c) True. Since line AE_2 shows the price level at full employment, any increase in spending above this line will result in inflation.

Questions

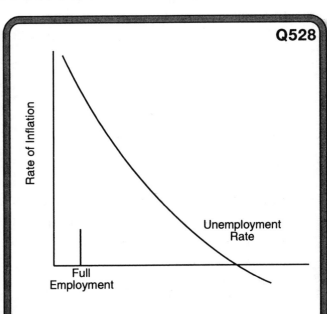

The Phillips Curve

a) **True or False:** The Phillips Curve figure above shows that as the rate of inflation decreases, unemployment also decreases.

b) **True or False:** The Phillips Curve figure above shows that policies of the government or of the Federal Reserve System that reduce unemployment have a cost in terms of higher inflation.

c) **True or False:** The Phillips Curve figure above shows that inflationary problems can begin only after an economy reaches full employment.

Your Own Answers _____

_____

_____

Correct Answers

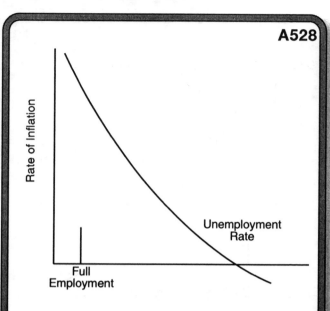

The Phillips Curve

a) False. It shows that as the rate of inflation decreases, unemployment increases.

b) True. If the government spends more money to hire the unemployed, this will increase the money supply and velocity, and will lead to some inflation.

c) False. It shows that inflationary problems can begin even before an economy reaches full employment.

BLANK CARDS
To Make Up Your Own Questions

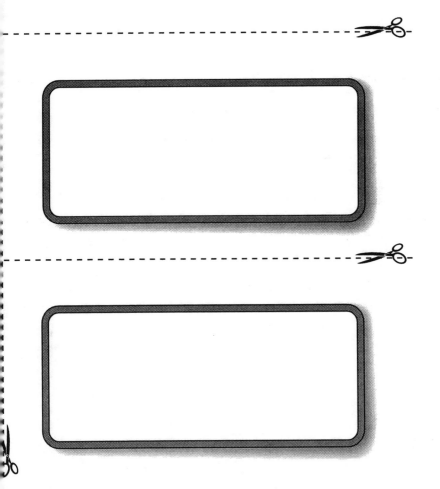

CORRECT ANSWERS

for

Your Own Questions

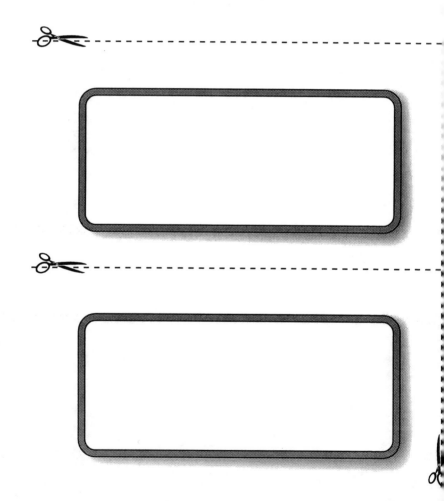

Blank Cards for
Your Own Questions

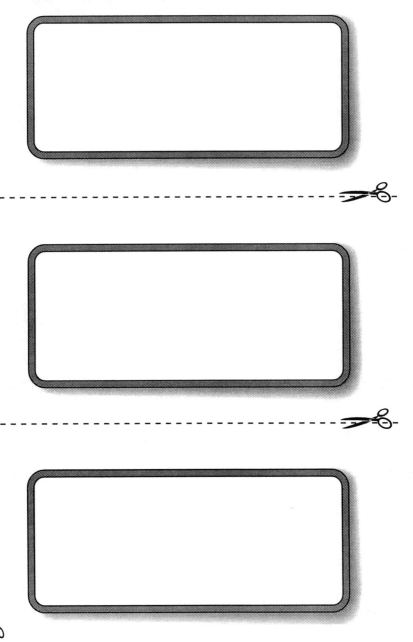

Correct Answers

Blank Cards for *Your Own Questions*

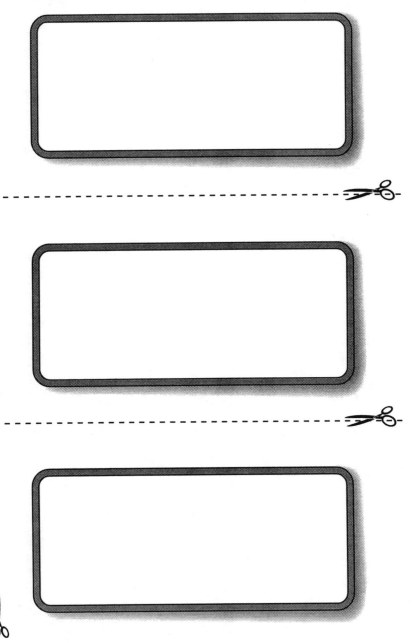

Correct Answers

Blank Cards for *Your Own Questions*

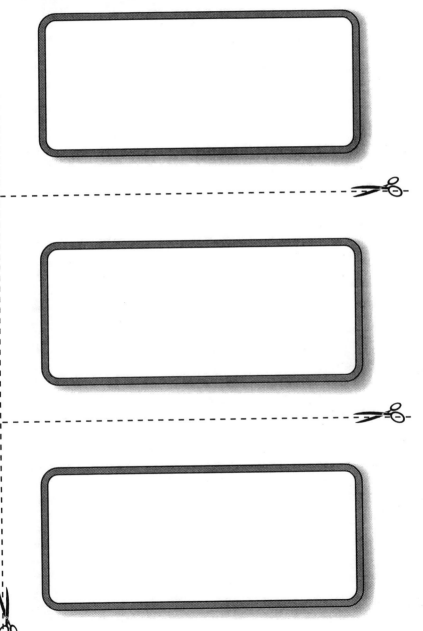

Correct Answers

Blank Cards for
Your Own Questions

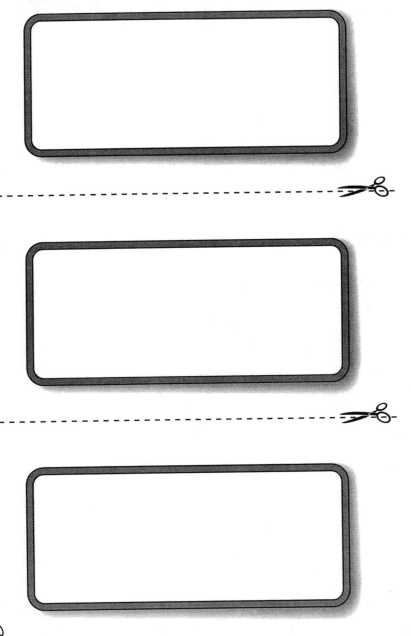

Correct Answers

Blank Cards for
Your Own Questions

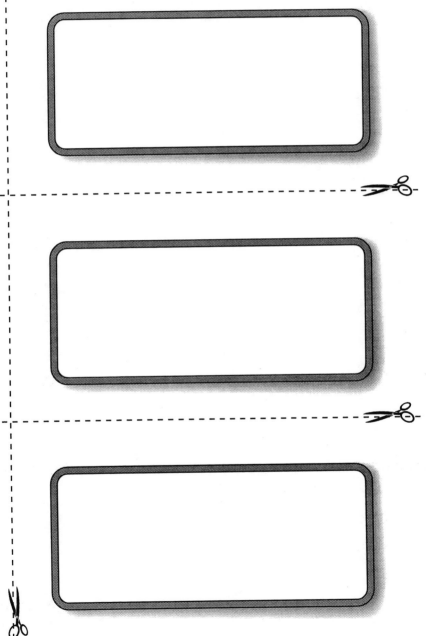

Correct Answers

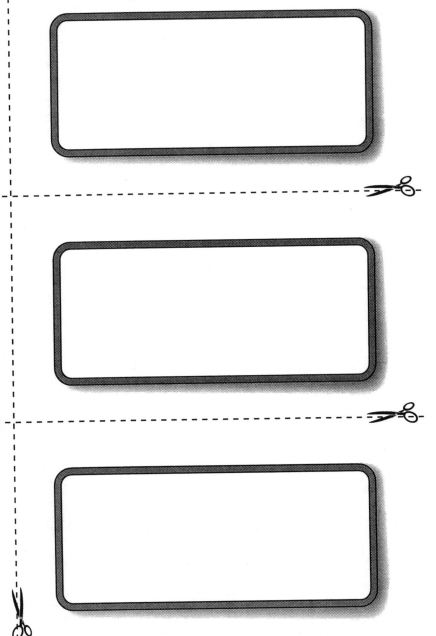

Blank Cards for
Your Own Questions

Correct Answers

Blank Cards for
Your Own Questions

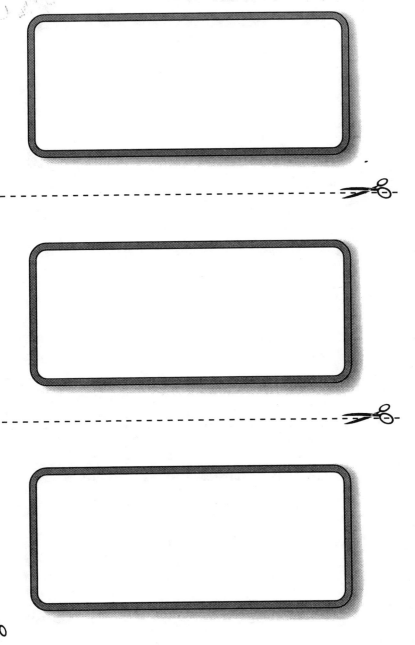

Correct Answers

Blank Cards for *Your Own Questions*

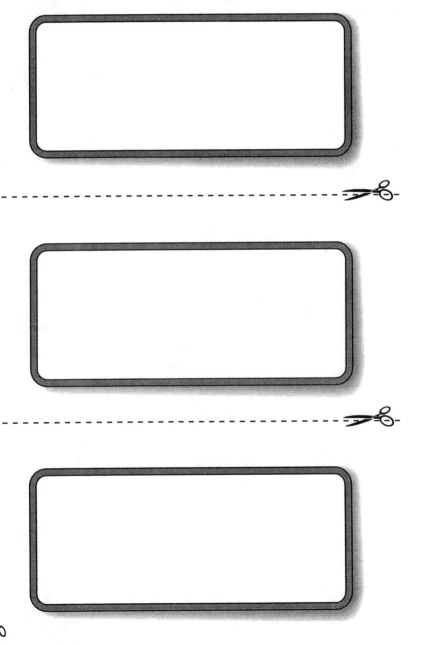

Correct Answers

Blank Cards for *Your Own Questions*

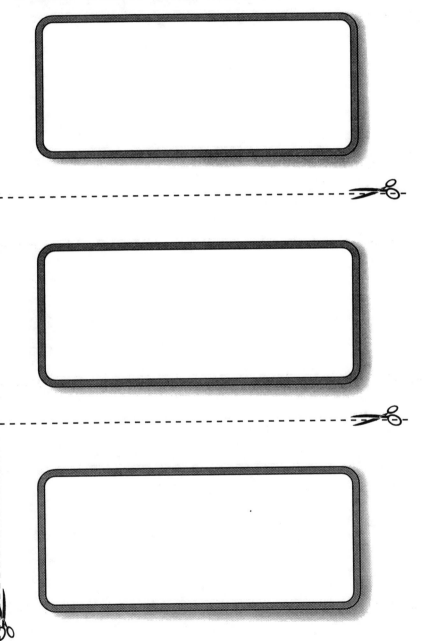

Correct Answers

Blank Cards for *Your Own Questions*

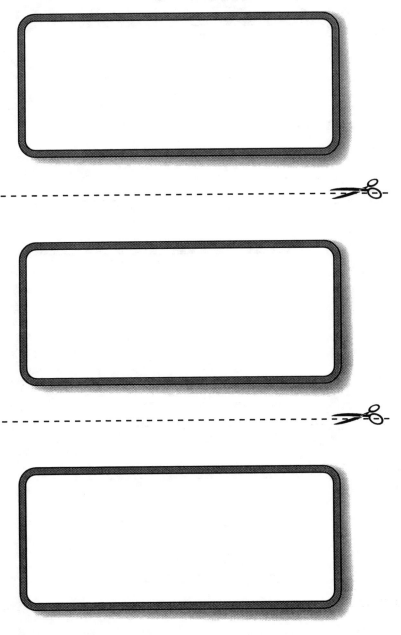

Correct Answers

Blank Cards for *Your Own Questions*

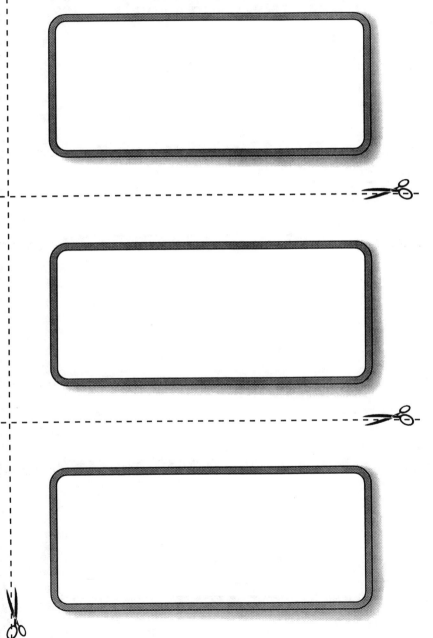

Correct Answers

Blank Cards for
Your Own Questions

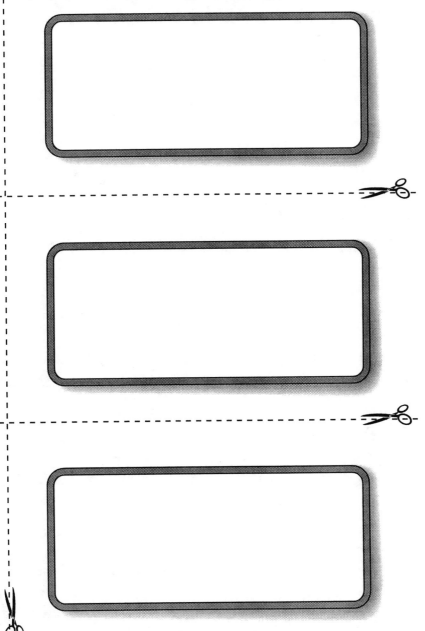

Correct Answers

Blank Cards for
Your Own Questions

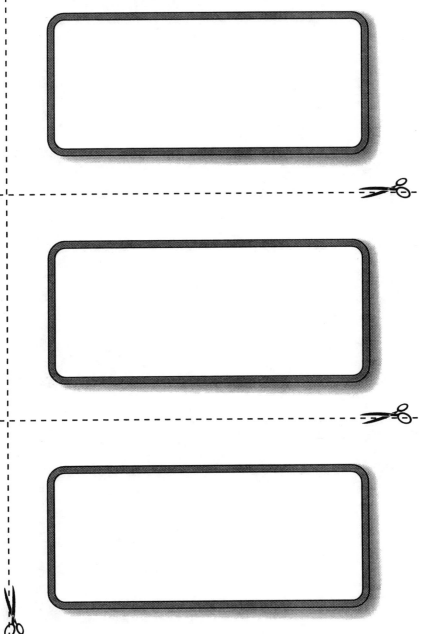

Correct Answers

Blank Cards for *Your Own Questions*

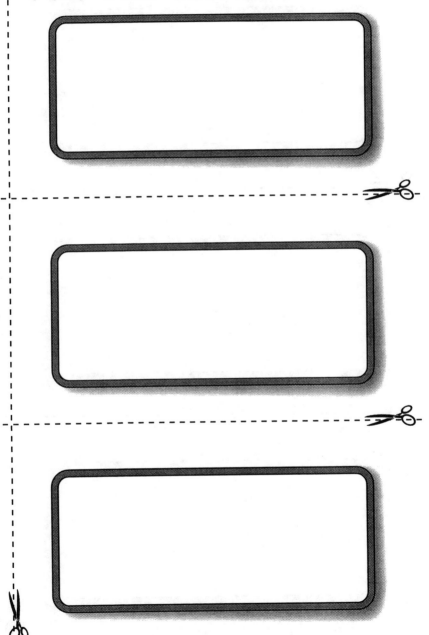

Correct Answers

Blank Cards for
Your Own Questions

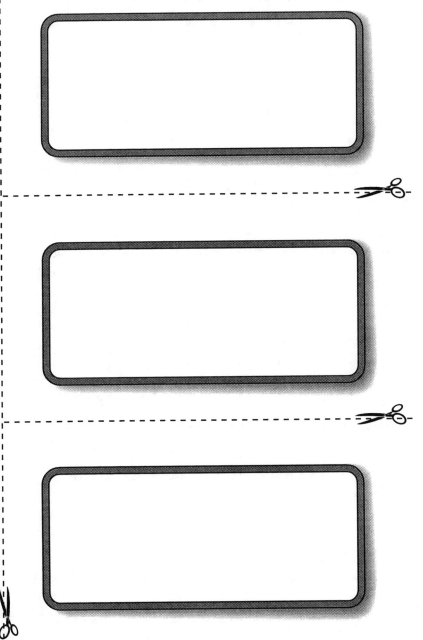

Correct Answers

Blank Cards for
Your Own Questions

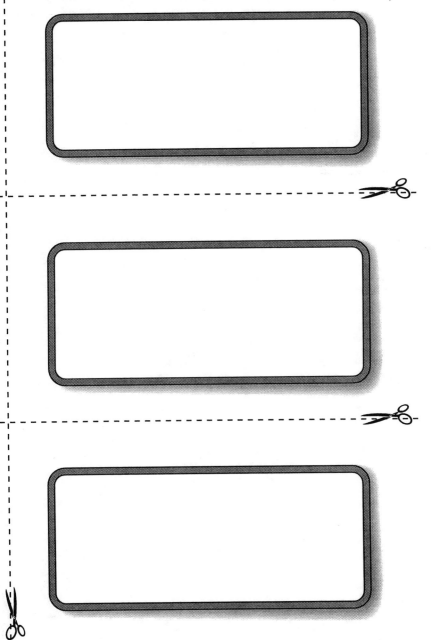

Correct Answers

Blank Cards for *Your Own Questions*

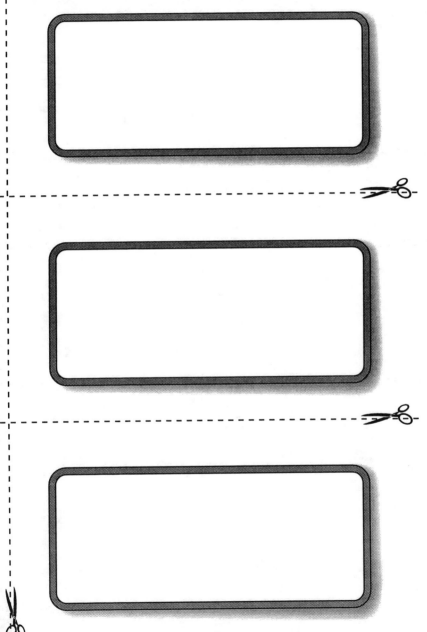

Correct Answers

Blank Cards for
Your Own Questions

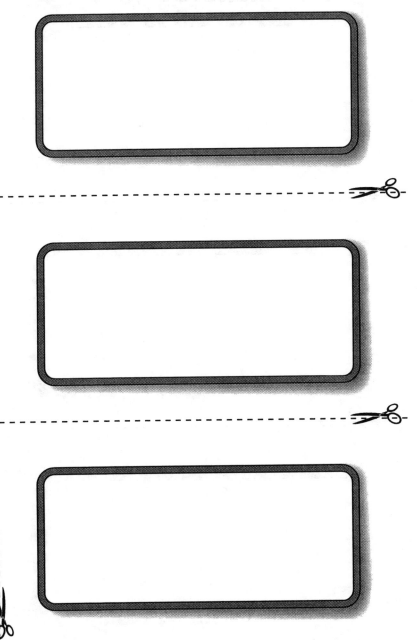

Correct Answers

Blank Cards for *Your Own Questions*

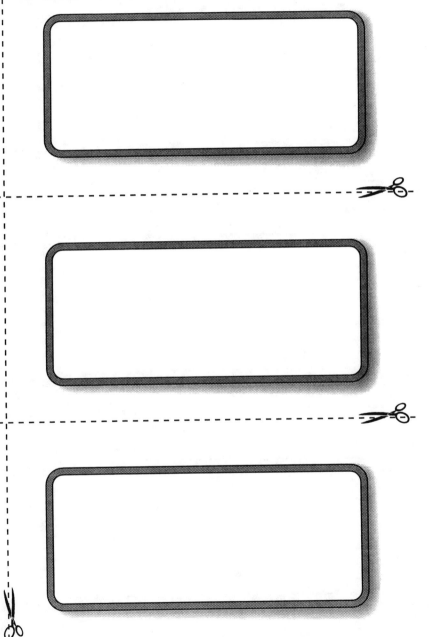

Correct Answers

Blank Cards for
Your Own Questions

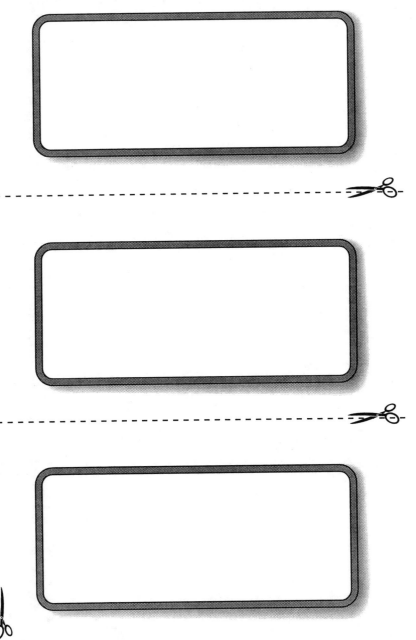

Correct Answers

Blank Cards for *Your Own Questions*

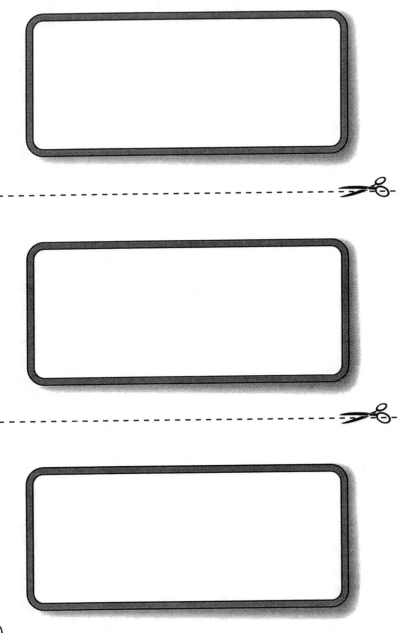

Correct Answers

INDEX